THE END OF THE END OF THE EARTH

OF THE EARTH   ESSAYS

JONATHAN FRANZEN

4th ESTATE • London

4th Estate
An imprint of HarperCollins*Publishers*
1 London Bridge Street
London SE1 9GF

www.4thEstate.co.uk

First published in Great Britain in 2018 by 4th Estate
First published in the United States by Farrar, Straus & Giroux in 2018

1

For their help with these essays, the author thanks Will Akers,
Ernesto Barbieri, Henry Finder, Adrian Forsyth, Susan Golomb,
Pilar Guzmán, Casey Lott, Etleva Pushi, Jamie Shreeve, and Nell Zink.

ISBN 978-0-00-829922-4 (hardback)
ISBN 978-0-00-829923-1 (trade paperback)

Designed by Abby Kagan

Printed and bound in Great Britain by
CPI Group (UK) Ltd, Croydon,CR0 4YY

MIX
Paper from
responsible sources
FSC
www.fsc.org
FSC C007454

This book is produced from independently certified FSC paper
to ensure responsible forest management.

For more information visit: www.harpercollins.co.uk/green

To Kathy, again,
and in memory of Martin Schneider-Jacoby
and Mindy Baha El Din

CONTENTS

THE ESSAY IN DARK TIMES

I f an essay is something *essayed*—something hazarded, not definitive, not authoritative; something ventured on the basis of the author's personal experience and subjectivity—we might seem to be living in an essayistic golden age. Which party you went to on Friday night, how you were treated by a flight attendant, what your take on the political outrage of the day is: the presumption of social media is that even the tiniest subjective micronarrative is worthy not only of private notation, as in a diary, but of sharing with other people. The U.S. president now operates on this presumption. Traditionally hard-news reporting, in places like *The New York Times*, has softened up to allow the I, with its voice and opinions and impressions, to take the front-page spotlight, and book reviewers feel less and less constrained to discuss books with any kind of objectivity. It didn't use to matter if Raskolnikov and Lily Bart were likable, but the question of "likability," with its implicit privileging of the reviewer's personal feelings, is now a key element of critical judgment. And literary fiction itself is looking more and more like essay. Some of the most influential novels of recent years, by Rachel Cusk and Karl Ove Knausgaard, take the method of self-conscious first-person testimony to a new level. Their more extreme admirers will tell you that imagination and invention are outmoded contrivances; that to inhabit the subjectivity of a character unlike the author is an act of appropriation, even colonialism; that the only authentic and politically defensible mode of narrative is autobiography.

Meanwhile the personal essay itself—the formal apparatus of honest self-examination and sustained engagement with ideas, as developed by Montaigne and advanced by Emerson and Woolf and Baldwin—is in eclipse. Most large-circulation American magazines have all but ceased to publish pure essays. The form persists mainly in smaller publications that collectively have fewer readers than Margaret Atwood has Twitter followers. Should we be mourning the essay's extinction? Or should we be celebrating its conquest of the larger culture?

A personal and subjective micronarrative: The few lessons I've learned about writing essays all came from my editor at *The New Yorker*, Henry Finder. I first went to Henry, in 1994, as a would-be journalist in pressing need of money. Largely through dumb luck, I produced a publishable article about the U.S. Postal Service, and then, through native incompetence, I wrote an unpublishable piece about the Sierra Club. This was the point at which Henry suggested that I might have some aptitude as an essayist. I heard him to be saying, "since you're obviously a crap journalist," and denied that I had any such aptitude. I'd been raised with a Midwestern horror of yakking too much about myself, and I had an additional prejudice, derived from certain wrongheaded ideas about novel-writing, against the *stating* of things that could more rewardingly be *depicted*. But I still needed money, so I kept calling Henry for book-review assignments. On one of these calls, he asked me if I had any interest in the tobacco industry—the subject of a major new history by Richard Kluger. I quickly said: "Cigarettes are the last thing in the world I want to think about." To this, Henry even more quickly replied: "*Therefore* you must write about them."

This was my first lesson from Henry, and it remains the most important one. After smoking throughout my twenties, I'd succeeded in quitting for two years in my early thirties. But when I was assigned the post-office piece, and became terrified of picking up the phone and introducing myself as a *New Yorker* journalist, I'd taken up the habit again. In the years since then, I'd managed to think of myself as a nonsmoker, or at least as a person so firmly resolved to quit again that I might as well already have been a nonsmoker, even as I continued to smoke. My state of mind was like a quantum wave function in which I could be totally a smoker but also totally not a smoker, so long as I never took measure of myself. And it was instantly clear to me that writing about cigarettes would force me to take my measure. This is what essays do.

There was also the problem of my mother, whose father had died of lung cancer, and who was militantly anti-tobacco. I'd concealed my habit from her for more than fifteen years. One reason I needed to preserve my indeterminacy as a smoker/nonsmoker was that I didn't enjoy lying to her. As soon as I could succeed in quitting again, permanently, the wave function would collapse and I would be, one hundred percent, the non-smoker I'd always represented myself to be—but only if I didn't first come out, in print, as a smoker.

Henry had been a twentysomething wunderkind when Tina Brown hired him at *The New Yorker*. He had a distinctive tight-chested manner of speaking, a kind of hyperarticulate mumble, like prose acutely well edited but barely legible. I was awed by his intelligence and his erudition and had quickly come to live in fear of disappointing him. His passionate emphasis in "*Therefore* you must write about them"—he was the only speaker I knew who could get away with the stressed initial "*Therefore*" and the imperative "must"—allowed me to hope that I'd registered in his consciousness in some small way.

And so I went to work on the essay, every day combusting half a dozen low-tar cigarettes in front of a box fan in my living-room window, and handed in the only thing I ever wrote for Henry that didn't need his editing. I don't remember how my mother got her hands on the essay or how she conveyed to me her deep sense of betrayal, whether by letter or in a phone call, but I do remember that she then didn't communicate with me for six weeks—by a wide margin, the longest she ever went silent on me. It was exactly as I'd feared. But when she got over it and began sending me letters again, I felt seen by her, seen for what I was, in a way I'd never felt before. It wasn't just that my "real" self had been concealed from her; it was as if there hadn't really been a self to see.

Kierkegaard, in *Either/Or*, makes fun of the "busy man" for whom busyness is a way of avoiding an honest self-reckoning. You might wake up in the night and realize that you're lonely in your marriage, or that you need to think about what your level of consumption is doing to the planet, but the next day you have a million little things to do, and the day after that you have another million things. As long as there's no end of little things, you never have to stop and confront the bigger questions. Writing or reading an essay isn't the only way to stop and ask yourself who you really are and what your life might mean, but it is one good way. And if you consider how laughably unbusy Kierkegaard's Copenhagen was, compared with our own age, those subjective tweets and hasty blog posts don't seem so essay-istic. They seem more like a means of avoiding what a real essay might force on us. We spend our days reading, on screens, stuff we'd never bother reading in a printed book, and bitch about how busy we are.

I quit cigarettes for the second time in 1997. And then, in 2002, for the final time. And then, in 2003, for the last and final time—unless you count the smokeless nicotine that's coursing through my bloodstream as I write this. Attempting to write an honest essay doesn't alter the multiplicity of my selves; I'm still simultaneously a reptile-brained addict, a worrier about my health, an eternal teenager, a self-medicating depressive. What changes, if I take the time to stop and measure, is that my multi-selved identity acquires *substance*.

One of the mysteries of literature is that personal substance, as perceived by both the writer and the reader, is situated outside the body of either of them, on some kind of page. How can I feel realer to myself in a thing I'm writing than I do inside my body? How can I feel closer to another person when I'm reading her words than I do when I'm sitting next to her? The answer, in part, is that both writing and reading demand full attentiveness. But it surely also has to do with the kind of *ordering* that is possible only on the page.

Here I might mention two other lessons I learned from Henry Finder. One was *Every essay, even a think piece, tells a story.* The other was *There are only two ways to organize material: "Like goes with like" and "This followed that."* These precepts may seem self-evident, but any grader of high-school or college essays can tell you that they aren't. To me it was especially not evident that a think piece should follow the rules of drama. And yet: Doesn't a good argument begin by positing some difficult problem? And doesn't it then propose an escape from the problem through some bold proposition, and set up obstacles in the form of objections and counterarguments, and finally, through a series of reversals, take us to an unforeseen but satisfying conclusion?

If you accept Henry's premise that a successful prose piece consists of material arranged in the form of a story, and if you share my own conviction that our identities consist of the stories we tell about ourselves, it makes sense that we should get a strong hit of personal substance from the labor of writing and the pleasure of reading. When I'm alone in the woods or having dinner with a friend, I'm overwhelmed by the quantity of random sensory data coming at me. The act of writing subtracts almost everything, leaving only the alphabet and punctuation marks, and progresses toward nonrandomness. Sometimes, in ordering the elements of a familiar story, you discover that it doesn't mean what you thought it did. Sometimes, especially with an argument ("This follows *from* that"), a completely new narrative is called for. The discipline of fashioning a compelling story can crystallize thoughts and feelings you only dimly knew you had in you.

If you're looking at a mass of material that doesn't seem to lend itself to storytelling, Henry would say your only other option is to sort it into categories, grouping similar elements together: *Like goes with like.* This is, at a minimum, a tidy way to write. But patterns also have a way of turning into stories. To make sense of Donald Trump's victory in an election he was widely expected to lose, it's tempting to construct a this-followed-that story: Hillary Clinton was careless with her emails, the Justice Department chose not to prosecute her, then Anthony Weiner's emails came to light, then James Comey reported to Congress that Clinton might still be in trouble, and then Trump won the election. But it may actually be more fruitful to group like with like: Trump's victory was *like* the Brexit vote and *like* the resurgent anti-immigrant nationalism in Europe. Clinton's imperiously sloppy handling of her emails was like her poorly messaged campaign and like her decision not to campaign harder in Michigan and Pennsylvania.

I was in Ghana on Election Day, birdwatching with my brother and two friends. James Comey's report to Congress had unsettled the campaign before I left for Africa, but Nate Silver's authoritative polling website, FiveThirtyEight, was still giving Trump just a thirty percent chance of winning. Having cast an early ballot for Clinton, I'd arrived in Accra feeling only moderately anxious about the election and congratulating myself on my decision to spend the final week of the campaign not checking FiveThirtyEight ten times a day.

I was indulging a different sort of compulsion in Ghana. To my shame, I am what people in the world of birding call a lister. It's not that I don't love birds for their own sake. I go birding to experience their beauty and diversity, learn more about their behavior and the ecosystems they belong to, and take long, attentive walks in new places. But I also keep way too many lists. I count not only the bird species I've seen worldwide but the ones I've seen in every country and every U.S. state I've birded in, also at various smaller sites, including my back yard, and in every calendar year since 2003. I can rationalize my compulsive counting as an extra little game I play within the context of my passion. But I really am compulsive. This makes me morally inferior to birders who bird exclusively for the joy of it.

It happened that by going to Ghana I'd given myself a chance to break my previous year-list record of 1,286 species. I was already over 800 for 2016, and I knew, from my online research, that trips similar to ours had produced nearly 500 species, only a handful of which are also common in America. If I could see 460 unique year species in Africa, and then use my seven-hour layover in London to pick up twenty easy European birds at a park near Heathrow, 2016 would be my best year ever.

We were seeing great stuff in Ghana, spectacular turacos and bee-eaters found only in West Africa. But the country's few remaining forests are under intense hunting and logging pressure, and our walks in them were more sweltering than productive. By the evening of Election Day, we'd already missed our only shot at several of my target species. Very early the next morning, when polls were still open on the West Coast of the States, I turned on my phone for the pleasure of confirming that Clinton was winning the election. What I found instead were stricken texts from my friends in California, with pictures of them staring at a TV and looking morose, my girlfriend curled up on a sofa in a fetal position. The *Times* headline of the moment was "Trump Takes North Carolina, Building Momentum; *Clinton's Path to Victory Narrow.*"

There was nothing to be done but go birding. On a road in the Nsuta Forest, dodging timber trucks whose momentum I associated with Trump's, and yet clinging to the idea that Clinton still had a path to victory, I saw Black Dwarf Hornbills, an African Cuckoo-Hawk, and a Melancholy Woodpecker.* It

*I am following standard ornithological practice and capitalizing the American names of birds when discussing them as species. Many woodpeckers could be described as melancholy, but there is only one species called Melancholy Woodpecker.

was a sweaty but satisfactory morning that ended, when we re-emerged into network coverage, with the news that the "short-fingered vulgarian" (*Spy* magazine's memorable epithet) was my country's new president. This was the moment when I saw what my mind had been doing with Nate Silver's figure of thirty percent for Trump's odds. Somehow I'd taken the figure to mean that the world might be, worst-case, thirty percent shittier after Election Day. What the number actually represented, of course, was a thirty percent chance of the world's being one hundred percent shittier.

As we traveled up into drier, emptier northern Ghana, we intersected with some birds I'd long dreamed of seeing: Egyptian Plovers, Carmine Bee-eaters, and a male Standard-winged Nightjar, whose outrageous wing streamers gave it the look of a nighthawk being closely pursued by two bats. But we were falling ever farther behind the year-bird pace I needed to maintain. It occurred to me, belatedly, that the trip lists I'd seen online had included species that were only heard, not seen, while I needed to see a bird to count it. Those lists had raised my hopes the way Nate Silver had. Now every target species I missed increased the pressure to see all of the remaining targets, even the wildly unlikely ones, if I wanted to break my record. It was only a stupid year list, ultimately meaningless even to me, but I was haunted by the headline from the morning after Election Day. Instead of 275 electoral votes, I needed 460 species, and my path to victory was becoming very narrow. Finally, four days before the end of the trip, in the spillway of a dam near the Burkina Faso border, where I'd hoped to get half a dozen new grassland birds and saw zero, I had to accept the reality of loss. I was suddenly aware that I should have been at home, trying to console my girlfriend about the election, exercising the one benefit of being a depressive pessimist, which is the propensity to laugh in dark times.

How had the short-fingered vulgarian reached the White House? When Hillary Clinton started speaking in public again, she lent credence to a like-goes-with-like account of her character by advancing a this-followed-that narrative. Never mind that she'd mishandled her emails and uttered the phrase "basket of deplorables." Never mind that voters might have had legitimate grievances with the liberal elite she represented; might have failed to appreciate the rationality of free trade, open borders, and factory automation when the overall gains in global wealth came at middle-class expense; might have resented the federal imposition of liberal urban values on conservative rural communities. According to Clinton, her loss was the fault of James Comey—maybe also of the Russians.

Admittedly, I had my own neat narrative account. When I came home from Africa to Santa Cruz, my progressive friends were still struggling to understand how Trump could have won. I remembered a public event I'd once done with the optimistic social-media specialist Clay Shirky, who'd recounted to the audience how "shocked" professional New York restaurant critics had been when Zagat, a crowdsourced reviewing service, had named Union Square Cafe the best restaurant in town. Shirky's point was that professional critics aren't as smart as they think they are; that, in fact, in the age of Big Data, critics are no longer even necessary. At the event, ignoring the fact that Union Square Cafe was *my* favorite New York restaurant (the crowd was right!), I'd sourly wondered if Shirky believed that critics were also stupid to consider Alice Munro a better writer than James Patterson. But now

Trump's victory, too, had vindicated Shirky's mockery of pundits. Social media had allowed Trump to bypass the critical establishment, and just enough members of the crowd, in key swing states, had found his low comedy and his incendiary speech "better" than Clinton's nuanced arguments and her mastery of policy. *This follows from that*: without Twitter and Facebook, no Trump.

After the election, Mark Zuckerberg did briefly seem to take responsibility, sort of, for having created the platform of choice for fake news about Clinton, and to suggest that Facebook could become more active in filtering the news. (Good luck with that.) Twitter, for its part, kept its head down. As Trump's tweeting continued unabated, what could Twitter possibly say? That it was making the world a better place?

In December, my favorite Santa Cruz radio station, KPIG, began running a fake ad offering counseling services to addicts of Trump-hating tweets and Facebook posts. The following month, a week before Trump's inauguration, the PEN American Center organized events around the country to reject the assault on free speech that it claimed Trump represented. Although his administration's travel restrictions did later make it harder for writers from Muslim countries to have their voices heard in the United States, the one bad thing that could *not* be said of Trump, in January, was that he had in any way curtailed free speech. His lying, bullying tweets were free speech on steroids. PEN itself, just a few years earlier, had given a free-speech award to Twitter, for its self-publicized role in the Arab Spring. The actual result of the Arab Spring had been a retrenchment of autocracy, and Twitter had since revealed itself, in Trump's hands, to be a platform made to order for autocracy, but the ironies didn't end there. During the same week in January, progressive American bookstores and authors proposed a boycott of Simon &

Schuster for the crime of intending to publish one book by the dismal right-wing provocateur Milo Yiannopoulos. The angriest of the bookstores talked of refusing to stock *all* titles from S&S, including, presumably, the books of Andrew Solomon, the president of PEN. The talk didn't end until S&S voided its contract with Yiannopoulos.

Trump and his alt-right supporters take pleasure in pushing the buttons of the politically correct, but it only works because the buttons are there to be pushed—students and activists claiming the right to not hear things that upset them, and to shout down ideas that offend them. Intolerance particularly flourishes online, where measured speech is punished by not getting clicked on, invisible Facebook and Google algorithms steer you toward content you agree with, and nonconforming voices stay silent for fear of being flamed or trolled or unfriended. The result is a silo in which, whatever side you're on, you feel absolutely right to hate what you hate. And here is another way in which the essay differs from superficially similar kinds of subjective speech. The essay's roots are in literature, and literature at its best—the work of Alice Munro, for example—invites you to ask whether you might be somewhat wrong, maybe even entirely wrong, and to imagine why someone else might hate you.

Three years ago, I was in a state of rage about climate change. The Republican Party was continuing to lie about the absence of a scientific consensus on climate—Florida's Department of Environmental Protection had gone so far as to forbid its employees to write the words *climate change*, after Florida's governor, a Republican, insisted that it wasn't a "true fact"—but I wasn't much less angry at the left. I'd read a new book by Naomi Klein, *This Changes Everything*, in which she assured the reader that, although "time is tight," we still have ten years to radically remake the global economy and prevent global temperatures from rising by more than two degrees Celsius by the end of the century. Klein's optimism was touching, but it, too, was a kind of denialism. Even before the election of Donald Trump, there was no evidence to suggest that humanity is capable—politically, psychologically, ethically, economically—of slashing carbon emissions quickly and deeply enough to change everything. Even the European Union, which had taken the early lead on climate, and was fond of lecturing other regions on their irresponsibility, needed only a recession in 2009 to shift its focus to economic growth. Barring a worldwide revolt against free-market capitalism in the next ten years—the scenario that Klein contended could still save us—the most *likely* rise in temperature this century is on the order of six degrees. We'll be lucky to avoid a two-degree rise before the year 2030.

In a polity ever more starkly divided, the truth about global warming was even less convenient to the left than to the right. The right's denials were odious lies, but at least they were consistent with a certain cold-eyed political realism. The left, having excoriated the right for its intellectual dishonesty and turned climate denialism into a political rallying cry, was now in an impossible position. It had to keep insisting on the truth of climate science while persisting in the fiction that collective world action could stave off the worst of it: that universal acceptance of the facts, which really might have changed everything in 1995, could still change everything. Otherwise, what difference did it make if the Republicans quibbled with the science?

Because my sympathies were with the left—reducing carbon

emissions is vastly better than doing nothing; every half degree helps—I also held it to a higher standard. Denying the dark reality, pretending that the Paris Accord could avert catastrophe, was understandable as a tactic to keep people motivated to reduce emissions; to keep hope alive. As a strategy, though, it did more harm than good. It ceded the ethical high ground, insulted the intelligence of unpersuaded voters ("Really? We still have ten years?"), and precluded frank discussion of how the global community should prepare for drastic changes, and how nations like Bangladesh should be compensated for what nations like the United States have done to them.

Dishonesty also skewed priorities. In the past twenty years, the environmental movement had become captive to a single issue. Partly out of genuine alarm, partly also because foregrounding human problems was politically less risky—less elitist—than talking about nature, the big environmental NGOs had all invested their political capital in fighting climate change, a problem with a human face. The NGO that particularly enraged me, as a bird lover, was the National Audubon Society, once an uncompromising defender of birds, now a lethargic institution with a very large PR department. In September 2014, with much fanfare, that PR department had announced to the world that climate change was the number-one threat to the birds of North America. The announcement was both narrowly dishonest, because its wording didn't square with the conclusions of Audubon's own scientists, and broadly dishonest, because not one single bird death could be directly attributed to human carbon emissions. In 2014, the most serious threats to American birds were habitat loss and outdoor cats. By invoking the buzzword of climate change, Audubon got a lot of attention in the liberal media; another point had been scored against the science-denying right. But it was not at all clear how this helped birds. The only practical effect of Audubon's announce-ment, it seemed to me, was to discourage people from addressing the real threats to nature in the present.

I was so angry that I decided that I'd better write an essay. I began with a jeremiad against the National Audubon Society, broadened it into a scornful denunciation of the environmental movement generally, and then started waking up in the night in a panic of remorse and doubt. For the writer, an essay is a mirror, and I didn't like what I was seeing in this one. Why was I excoriating fellow liberals when the denialists were so much worse? The prospect of climate change was every bit as sickening to me as to the groups I was attacking. With every additional degree of global warming, further hundreds of millions of people around the world would suffer. Wasn't it worth an all-out effort to achieve a reduction of even half of one degree? Wasn't it obscene to be talking about birds when children in Bangladesh were threatened? Yes, the premise of my essay was that we have an ethical responsibility to other species as well as to our own. But what if that premise was false? And, even if it was true, did I really care personally about biodiversity? Or was I just a privileged white guy who liked to go birding? And not even a pure-hearted birder—a lister!

After three nights of doubting my character and motives, I called Henry Finder and told him I couldn't write the piece. I'd done plenty of ranting about climate to my friends and to like-minded conservationists, but it was like a lot of the ranting that happens online, where you're protected by the impromptu nature of the writing and by the known friendliness of your audience. Trying to write a finished thing, an essay, had made me aware of the sloppiness of my thinking. It had also enormously increased the risk of shame, because the writing wasn't casual, and because it was going out to an audience of probably hostile strangers. Following Henry's admonition ("*Therefore*"), I'd come to think of the essayist as a firefighter, whose job, while everyone else is fleeing the flames of shame, is to run straight into them. But I had a lot more to fear now than my mother's disapproval.

My essay might have stayed abandoned if I hadn't already clicked a button on Audubon's website, affirming that, yes, I wanted to join it in fighting climate change. I'd only done this to gather rhetorical ammunition to use against Audubon, but a deluge of direct-mail solicitations had followed from that click. I got at least eight of them in six weeks, all of them asking me to give money, along with a similar deluge in my email in-box. A few days after speaking to Henry, I opened one of the emails and found myself looking at a picture of *myself*—luckily a flattering image, taken in 2010 for *Vogue* magazine, which had dressed me up better than I dress myself and posed me in a field with my binoculars, like a birder. The headline of the email was something like "Join Author Jonathan Franzen in Supporting Audubon." It was true that, a few years earlier, in an interview with *Audubon* magazine, I'd politely praised the organization, or at least its magazine. But no one had asked for my permission to use my name and image for solicitation. I wasn't sure the email was even legal.

A more benign impetus to return to the essay came from Henry. As far as I know, Henry couldn't care less about birds, but he seemed to see something in my argument that our preoccupation with future catastrophes discourages us from tackling solvable environmental problems in the here and now. In an email to me, he gently suggested that I lose the tone of prophetic scorn. "This piece will be more persuasive," he wrote in another, "if, ironically, it's more ambivalent, less polemical. You're not whaling on folks who want us to pay attention to climate change and emission reductions. But you're attentive to the costs. To what the discourse pushes to the margins." Email by email, revision by revision, Henry nudged me toward framing the essay not as a denunciation but as a question: How do we find meaning in our actions when the world seems to be coming to an end? Much of the final draft was devoted to a pair of well-conceived regional conservation projects, in Peru and Costa Rica, where the world really is being made a better place, not just for wild plants and wild animals but for the Peruvians and Costa Ricans who live there. Work on these projects is personally meaningful, and the benefits are immediate and tangible.

In writing about the two projects, I hoped that one or two of the big charitable foundations, the ones spending tens of millions of dollars on biodiesel development or on wind farms in Eritrea, might read the piece and consider investing in work that produces tangible results. What I got instead was a missile attack from the liberal silo. I'm not on social media, but my friends reported that I was being called all sorts of names, including "birdbrain" and "climate-change denier." Tweet-size snippets of my essay, retweeted out of context, made it sound as if I'd proposed that we *abandon* the effort to reduce carbon emissions, which was the position of the Republican Party, which, by the polarizing logic of online discourse, made me a climate-change denier. In fact, I'm such a climate-science accepter that I don't even bother having hope for the ice caps. All I'd denied was that a right-minded international elite, meeting in nice hotels around the world, could stop them from melting. This was my crime against orthodoxy. Climate now has such a lock on the liberal imagination that any attempt to change the conversation—even trying to change it to the epic extinction event that human beings are already creating without the help of climate change—amounts to an offense against religion.

I did have sympathy for the climate-change professionals who denounced the essay. They'd been working for decades to raise the alarm in America, and they finally had President Obama on board with them; they had the Paris Accord. It was an inopportune time to point out that drastic global warming is already a done deal, and that it seems unlikely that humanity is going to leave any carbon in the ground, given that, even now, not one country in the world has pledged to do it. I also understood the fury of the alternative-energy industry, which is a business like any other. If you allow that renewable-energy projects are only a moderating tactic, unable to reverse the damage that past carbon emissions will continue to do for centuries, it opens the door to other questions about the business. Like, did we really need quite so many windmills? Did they have to be placed in ecologically sensitive areas? And the solar farms in the Mojave Desert—wouldn't it make more sense to cover the city of Los Angeles with solar panels and spare the open space? Weren't we sort of destroying the natural world in order to save it? I believe it was an industry blogger who called me a birdbrain.

As for Audubon, the fund-raising email should have warned me about the character of its management. But I was still surprised by its response to the essay, which was to attack, ad hominem, the person whose name and image it had blithely appropriated two months earlier. My essay had, yes, given Audubon some tough love. I wanted it to cut out the nonsense, stop talking about fifty years from now, and be more aggressive in defending the birds that both it and I love. But apparently all Audubon could see was a threat to its membership numbers and its fund-raising efforts, and so it had to negate me as a person.

I'm told the president of Audubon fired off four different salvos at me personally. This is what presidents do now.

And it worked. Without even reading those salvos—simply from knowing that other people were reading them—I felt ashamed. I felt the way I'd felt in eighth grade, shunned by the crowd and called names that shouldn't have hurt but did. I wished I'd listened to my panics in the night and kept my opinions to myself. In a state of some anguish, I called up Henry and dumped all my shame and regret on him. He replied, in his barely legible way, that the online response was only weather. "With public opinion," he said, "there's weather, and then there's climate. You're trying to change the climate, and that takes time."

It didn't matter if I believed this or not. It was enough to feel that one person, Henry, didn't hate me. I consoled myself with the thought that, although climate is too vast and chaotic for any individual to alter it, the individual can still find meaning in trying to make a difference to one afflicted village, one victim of global injustice. Or to one bird, or one reader. After the online flames had died down, I started hearing privately from conservation workers who shared my frustrations but couldn't afford to express them. I didn't hear from many people, but there didn't have to be many. My feeling in each case was the same: The person I wrote the essay for is you.

But now, two and a half years later, as ice shelves crumble and the Twitter president pulls out of the Paris Accord, I'm not so sure. Now I can admit to myself that I didn't write the essay just to hearten a few conservationists and deflect some charitable dollars to better causes. I really did want to change the climate.

I still do. I share, with the very people my essay criticized, the recognition that global warming is *the* issue of our time, perhaps the biggest issue in all of human history. Every one of us is now in the position of the indigenous Americans when the Europeans arrived with guns and smallpox: our world is poised to change vastly, unpredictably, and mostly for the worse. I don't have any hope that we can stop the change from coming. My only hope is that we can accept the reality in time to prepare for it humanely, and my only faith is that facing it honestly, however painful this may be, is better than denying it.

If I were writing the essay today, I might say all this. The mirror of the essay, as it was published, reflected an angry bird-loving misfit who thinks he's smarter than the crowd. That character may be me, but it's not the whole me, and a better essay would have reflected that. In a better essay, I might still have given Audubon the rebuke it deserved, but I would have found my way to more sympathy for the other people I was angry at: for the climate activists, who for twenty years had watched their path to victory narrow sickeningly, as carbon emissions mounted and the necessary emissions-reduction targets grew ever more unrealistic, and for the alternative-energy workers who had families to feed and were trying to see beyond petroleum, and for the environmental NGOs that thought they'd finally found an issue that could wake the world up, and for the leftists who, as neoliberalism and its technologies reduced the electorate to individual consumers, saw climate change as the last strong argument for collectivism. I would especially have tried to remember all the people who need more hope in their lives than a depressive pessimist does, the people for whom the prospect of a hot, calamity-filled future is unbearably sad and frightening, and who can be forgiven for not wanting to think about it. I would have kept revising.

MANHATTAN 1981

My girlfriend, V, and I were finishing college, with a summer to burn before the next thing, and New York beckoned. V went up to the city and signed a three-month lease on the apartment of a Columbia student, Bobby Atkins, who may have been the son of the creator of the Atkins Diet, or maybe we just enjoyed imagining that he was. His place, on the southwest corner of 110th Street and Amsterdam, had two small bedrooms and was irremediably filthy. We arrived in June with a fifth of Tanqueray, a carton of Marlboro Lights, and Marcella Hazan's Italian cookbook. Someone had left behind a spineless black plush-toy panther, manufactured in Korea, which we liberated and made ours.

We were living on a margin. Before full-scale gentrification, before mass incarceration, the city seemed starkly drawn in black and white. When a young Harlem humorist on the uptown 3 train performed the "magic" act of making every white passenger disappear at Ninety-sixth Street, I felt tried and found guilty of whiteness. Our friend Jon Justice, who that summer had Thomas Pynchon's *V* stuffed into the back pocket of his corduroys, was mugged at Grant's Tomb, where he shouldn't have been. I was aesthetically attracted to cities but morbidly afraid of being shot. In New York, Amsterdam Avenue was a sharp dividing line, and I stood on the east side of it only once, when I made the mistake of riding a C train to 110th and walking home from there. It was late afternoon and nobody paid attention to me, but I was light-headed with fear. Deepening my impression of menace were the heavy, light-blocking security gates on our windows and the police lock in our entry hall, its steel rod anchored to the floor and angling up to a slot on the front door. I associated it with our next-door neighbor, an elderly white man with raging senile dementia. He would pound on our door or stand on the landing, wearing only pajama bottoms, and asseverate, over and over, using a vile epithet, that his wife was having relations with black men. I was afraid of him, too, and I hated him for naming a racial division we liberal kids accepted in silence.

In theory, V and I were trying to write fiction, but I was oppressed by the summer heat and by the penitentiary gloom of the Atkins place, the cockroaches, the wandering neighbor. V and I fought, wept, made up, and played with our black panther. We practiced cooking and semiotic criticism and ventured out— always going west—to the Thalia, and Hunan Balcony, and Papyrus Books, where I bought the latest issue of *Semiotext(e)* and dense volumes of theory by Derrida and Kenneth Burke. I don't remember how I had any money at all. Conceivably my parents, despite their disapproval of New York and of my cohabitation with V, had given me some hundreds of dollars. I do remember sending letters to various magazines, inquiring about paid internships, and being told that I needed to have applied six months earlier.

Luckily, my brother Tom was in New York that summer, doing a loft conversion for the hotshot young photographer Gregory Heisler. Tom, who was then based in Chicago, had come east with a Chicago friend of Heisler's who wanted to start a renovation business and hoped to pick up some skills from my brother and split the profits. But Heisler could see that Tom had all the know-how. Before long, the friend was sent back to Chicago, leaving Tom without a laborer. This became my job.

Heisler was a portraitist, eventually best known for his double-exposed image of George H. W. Bush on the cover of *Time*. His loft was at the corner of Broadway and Houston, on the top floor of the Cable Building, then a den of sweatshops, later the home of the Angelika theater. The building was zoned for commercial use, and Tom and Heisler hadn't bothered with city permits, and so for me, at least, there was a frisson of illegality to the hidden apartment that Tom was building behind the photo studio's south wall. Heisler wanted every surface in the apartment covered with a trendy gray plastic laminate whose little raised dots made edging it with a router a nightmare. I spent long afternoons in a cloud of acetone fumes, cleaning rubber cement off the laminate, while Tom, in another room, cursed the raised dots.

My main job was to fetch things. Every morning, Tom gave me a shopping list of construction staples and exotica, and I made the rounds of supply stores on the Bowery and Canal Street. East of the Bowery were the dangerous alphabet streets and the projects, a zone of no-go on my mental map of the island. But in the rest of lower Manhattan I found the aesthetic experience I'd been looking for. SoHo's transformation was still larval, its streets quiet, its iron pillars peeling. Lower Broadway was peopled with garment workers, and the city below Canal seemed hungover from the seventies, as if the buildings were surprised to find themselves still standing. On the Fourth of July weekend, V and Jon Justice and I got up onto the old West Side Elevated Highway (closed but not yet demolished) and went walking under the new World Trade Center towers (brutalist but not yet tragic) and didn't see another person, white or black, in any direction.

Romantically deserted vistas were what I wanted in a city when I was twenty-one.

On the evening of the Fourth, when Morningside Heights began to sound like wartime Beirut, V and I went over to East End Avenue to watch the official fireworks from our friend Lisa Albert's family's apartment. I was astonished when her building's elevator opened directly into the apartment's front hall. Her family's cook asked me if I'd like a sandwich, and I said yes, please. It had never occurred to me that my background and Albert's weren't more or less the same. I hadn't imagined that an apartment like hers existed, or that a person only five years older than I was, Greg Heisler, could have a team of assistants at his disposal. He also had a willowy and dumbstrikingly beautiful wife, Pru, who came from Australia and wore airy white summer dresses that made me think of Daisy Buchanan.

The city's dividing line of wealth was not unrelated to the other dividing line, but it was less distinctly geographical and easier for me to cross. Under the spell of my elite college education, I envisioned overthrowing the capitalist political economy in the near future, through the application of literary theory, but in the meantime my education enabled me to feel at ease on the wealth side of the line. At the formal midtown restaurant where V's visiting grandmother took the two of us to lunch one day, I was given a blue blazer to wear with my black jeans, and this was all it took for me to pass.

I was too idealistic to want more money than I needed to subsist, too arrogant to envy Heisler, and so to me the rich were mainly a curiosity, interesting for the conspicuousness of both their consumption and their thrift. When V and I visited her other grandparents, at their country estate outside the city, they showed me the little paintings by Renoir and Cézanne in their living room and served us stale store-bought cookies. At Tavern on the Green, where we were taken to dinner by my brother Bob's in-laws, a pair of psychoanalysts who had an apartment not a lot smaller than Albert's, I was appalled to learn that if you wanted a vegetable with your steak you had to pay extra for it. The money seemed of no consequence to Bob's father-in-law, but we noticed that one of the mother-in-law's shoes was held together with electrical tape. Heisler, too, was given to grand gestures, like flying Tom's soon-to-be wife out from Chicago for a weekend. But he paid Tom $12,500 for the loft conversion, approximately one-eighth of what it would have cost with a New York contractor.

It was people like Tom and me who didn't recognize the value of what they had in hand. Tom realized too late that he could easily have charged Heisler two or three times as much, and I left Manhattan, in mid-August, owing $225 to St. Luke's Hospital. To celebrate the end of the summer and also, I think, our engagement to be married, V and I had gone to dinner at a Cuban restaurant on Columbus Avenue, Victor's, which her former boyfriend, a Cuban, had frequented. I started with black bean soup and was a few spoonfuls into it when the beans seemed to come alive on my tongue, churning with a kind of malevolent aggression. I reached into my mouth and pulled out a narrow shard of glass. V flagged down our server and complained to him. The server summoned the manager, who apologized, examined the piece of glass, disappeared with it, and then came back to hustle us out of the restaurant. I was pressing a napkin to my tongue to stanch the bleeding. At the front door, I asked if it was okay for me to keep the napkin. "Yes, yes," the manager said, shutting the door behind us. V and I hailed our only cab of the summer and went directly to St. Luke's, our neighborhood hospital. Eventually a doctor told me that my cut would heal quickly and did not require stitches, but I had to wait a couple of hours to receive this information and a tetanus shot. Directly across from me, in one of the corridors where I waited, a young African-American woman was lying on a gurney with a gunshot wound in her bared abdomen. The wound was leaking pinkish fluid but was evidently not life-threatening. I can still see it vividly, a .22-caliber-size hole, the thing I'd walked in fear of.

Fifteen years later, after being married and divorced, I built a work studio in a loft on 125th Street, following Tom's example and hanging my own drywall, wiring my own outlets. I'd gotten smarter about money, and I was able to jump on a cheap space in Harlem because I wasn't scared of the city anymore. I had a personal connection with the Harlemites in my building, and after work I could go downtown and safely walk with my friends on the alphabet streets, which were being colonized by young white people. In time, on the strength of the sales of the book I'd written in Harlem, I bought my own Upper East Side co-op and became a person who took younger friends and relatives to dinner at places they couldn't have afforded.

The city's dividing line had become more permeable, at least in one direction. White power had reasserted itself through the pressure of real-estate prices and police action. In hindsight, the era of white fear seems most remarkable for having lasted as long as it did. Of all my mistakes as a twenty-one-year-old in the city, the one I now regret the most was my failure to imagine that the black New Yorkers I was afraid of might be even more afraid than I was.

On my last full day in Manhattan that summer, I got a check from Greg Heisler for my last four weeks of work. To cash it, I had to go to the European American Bank, a strange little hexagonal building that sat on a bite of dismal parkland taken out of SoHo's southeast flank. I don't remember how many hundred-dollar bills I was given there—maybe it was six, maybe nine—but it seemed to me a dangerous amount of cash to carry in my wallet. Before I left the bank, I discreetly slipped the bills into one of my socks. Outside, it was one of those bright August mornings when a cold front flushes the badness from the city's sky. I headed straight to the nearest subway, anxious about my wealth, hoping I could pass as poor to someone who wanted the money in my sock more than I did.

WHY BIRDS MATTER

I f you could see every bird in the world, you'd see the whole world. Things with feathers can be found in every corner of every ocean and in land habitats so bleak that they're habitats for nothing else. Gray Gulls raise their chicks in Chile's Atacama Desert, one of the driest places on Earth. Emperor Penguins incubate their eggs in Antarctica in winter. Goshawks nest in the Berlin cemetery where Marlene Dietrich is buried, sparrows in Manhattan traffic lights, swifts in sea caves, vultures on Himalayan cliffs, chaffinches in Chernobyl. The only forms of life more widely distributed than birds are microscopic.

To survive in so many different habitats, the world's ten thousand or so bird species have evolved into a spectacular diversity of forms. They range in size from the ostrich, which can reach nine feet in height and is widespread in Africa, to the aptly named Bee Hummingbird, found only in Cuba. Their bills can be massive (pelicans, toucans), tiny (Weebills), or as long as the rest of their body (Sword-billed Hummingbirds). Some birds—the Painted Bunting in Texas, Gould's Sunbird in South Asia, the Rainbow Lorikeet in Australia—are gaudier than any flower. Others come in one of the nearly infinite shades of brown that tax the vocabulary of avian taxonomists: *rufous, fulvous, ferruginous, bran-colored, foxy.*

Birds are no less diverse behaviorally. Some are highly social, others anti. African queleas and flamingos gather in flocks of millions, and parakeets build whole parakeet cities out of sticks. Dippers walk alone and underwater, on the beds of mountain streams, and a Wandering Albatross may glide on its ten-foot wingspan five hundred miles away from any other albatrosses. New Zealand Fantails are friendly and may follow you on a trail. A caracara, if you stare at it too long, will swoop down and try to knock your head off. Roadrunners kill rattlesnakes for food by teaming up on them, one bird distracting the snake while another sneaks up behind it. Bee-eaters eat bees. Leaftossers toss leaves. The Oilbird, a unique nocturnal species of the American tropics, glides over avocado trees and snatches fruit on the fly; Snail Kites do the same thing, except with snails. Thick-billed Murres can dive underwater to a depth of 700 feet, Peregrine Falcons downward through the air at 240 miles an hour. A Wren-like Rushbird will spend its entire life beside one half-acre pond, while a Cerulean Warbler may migrate to Peru and then find its way back to the tree in New Jersey where it nested the year before.

Birds aren't furry and cuddly, but in many respects they're more similar to us than other mammals are. They build intricate homes and raise families in them. They take long winter vacations in warm places. Cockatoos are shrewd thinkers, solving puzzles that would challenge a chimpanzee, and crows like to play. (Check out the YouTube video of a crow in Russia sledding down a snowy roof on a plastic lid, flying back up with the lid in its beak, and sledding down again.) And then there are the songs with which birds, like us, fill the world. Nightingales trill in the suburbs of Europe, thrushes in downtown Quito, hwameis in Chengdu. Chickadees have a complex language for communicating, not only to one another but to every bird in their neighborhood, how safe or unsafe they feel from predators. Some lyrebirds in eastern Australia sing a tune their ancestors may have learned from a settler's flute nearly a century ago. If you shoot too many pictures of a lyrebird, it will add the sound of your camera to its repertoire.

But birds also do the thing we all wish we could do but can't, except in dreams: they fly. Eagles effortlessly ride thermals; hummingbirds pause in midair; quail burst into flight heart-stoppingly. Taken in sum, the flight paths of birds bind the planet together like a hundred billion filaments, tree to tree and continent to continent. There was never a time when the world seemed large to them. After breeding, a European swift will stay aloft for nearly a year, flying to sub-Saharan Africa and back, eating and molting and sleeping on the wing, without landing once. Young albatrosses spend as many as ten years roving the open ocean before they first return to land to breed. A Bar-tailed Godwit has been tracked flying nonstop from Alaska to New Zealand, 7,264 miles in nine days, while a Ruby-throated Hummingbird may burn up a third of its tiny body weight to cross the Gulf of Mexico. The Red Knot, a small shorebird species, makes annual round-trips between Tierra del Fuego and the Canadian Arctic; one long-lived individual, named B95 (for the tag on its leg), has flown more miles than separate the Earth and the moon.

There is, however, one critical ability that human beings have and birds do not: mastery of their environment. Birds can't protect wetlands, can't manage a fishery, can't air-condition their nests. They have only the instincts and the physical abilities that evolution has bequeathed them. These have served them well for a very long time, 150 million years longer than human beings have been around. But now human beings are changing the planet—its surface, its climate, its oceans—too quickly for birds to adapt by evolving. Crows and gulls may thrive at our garbage dumps, blackbirds and cowbirds at our feedlots, robins and bulbuls in our city parks. But the future of most bird species depends on our commitment to preserving them. Are they valuable enough for us to make the effort?

Value, in the late Anthropocene, has come almost exclusively to mean economic value, utility to human beings. And, certainly, many wild birds are usefully edible. Some of them in turn eat noxious insects and rodents. Many others perform vital roles—pollinating plants, spreading seeds, serving as food for mammalian predators—in ecosystems whose continuing wildness has touristic or carbon-sequestering value. You may also hear it argued that bird populations function, like the proverbial coal-mine canary, as important indicators of ecological health. But do we really need the absence of birds to tell us when a marsh is severely polluted, a forest slashed and burned, or a fishery destroyed? The sad fact is that wild birds, in themselves, will never pull their weight in the human economy. They want to eat our blueberries.

What bird populations do usefully indicate the health of is our *ethical* values. One reason that wild birds matter—ought to matter—is that they are our last, best connection to a natural world that is otherwise receding. They're the most vivid and widespread representatives of the Earth as it was before people arrived on it. They share descent with the largest animals ever to walk on land: the house finch outside your window is a tiny and beautifully adapted living dinosaur. A duck on your local pond looks and sounds very much like a duck twenty million years ago, in the Miocene epoch, when birds ruled the planet. In an ever more artificial world, where featherless drones fill the air and Angry Birds can be simulated on our phones, we may see no reasonable need to cherish and support the former rulers of the natural realm. But is economic calculation our highest standard? After Shakespeare's King Lear steps down from the throne, he pleads with his elder two daughters to grant him some vestige of his former majesty. When the daughters reply that they don't see the need for it, the old king bursts out: "O, reason not the need!" To consign birds to oblivion is to forget what we're the children of.

A person who says, "It's too bad about the birds, but human beings come first" is making one of two implicit claims. The person may mean that human beings are no better than any other animal—that our fundamentally self-centered selves, which are motivated by selfish genes, will always do whatever it takes to replicate our genes and maximize our pleasure, the nonhuman world be damned. This is the view of cynical realists, to whom a concern for other species is merely an annoying form of sentimentality. It's a view that can't be disproved, and it's available to anyone who doesn't mind admitting that he or she is hopelessly selfish.

But "human beings come first" may also have the opposite meaning: that our species is uniquely worthy of monopolizing the world's resources because we are *not* like other animals; because we have consciousness and free will, the capacity to remember our pasts and shape our futures. This opposing view can be found among both religious believers and secular humanists, and it, too, is neither provably true nor provably false. But it does raise the question: if we're incomparably more worthy than other animals, shouldn't our ability to discern right from wrong, and to knowingly sacrifice some small fraction of our convenience for a larger good, make us *more* susceptible to the claims of nature, rather than less? Doesn't a unique ability carry with it a unique responsibility?

If you stand in a forest in Southeast Asia, you may hear and then begin to feel, in your chest, a deep rhythmic whooshing. It sounds meteorological, but it's the wingbeats of Great Hornbills flying in to land in a fruiting tree. They have massive yellow bills and hefty white thighs; they look like a cross between a toucan and a giant panda. As they clamber around in the tree, placidly eating fruit, you may find yourself crying out with the rarest of all emotions: pure joy. It has nothing to do with what you want or what you possess. It's the sheer gorgeous fact of the Great Hornbill, which couldn't care less about you.

The radical otherness of birds is integral to their beauty and their value. They are always among us but never of us. They're the other world-dominating animals that evolution has produced, and their indifference to us ought to serve as a chastening reminder that we're not the measure of all things. The stories we tell about the past and imagine for the future are mental constructions that birds can do without. Birds live squarely in the present. And at present, although our cats and our windows and our pesticides kill billions of them every year, and although some species, particularly on oceanic islands, have been lost forever, their world is still very much alive. In every corner of the globe, in nests as small as walnuts or as large as haystacks, chicks are pecking through their shells and into the light.

SAVE WHAT YOU LOVE

Last September, as someone who cares more about birds than the next man, I was following the story of the new stadium the Twin Cities are building for their football Vikings. The stadium's glass walls were expected to kill thousands of birds every year, and local bird lovers had asked its sponsors to use a specially patterned glass to reduce collisions; the glass would have raised the stadium's cost by one-tenth of one percent, and the sponsors had balked. Around the same time, the National Audubon Society issued a press release declaring climate change "the greatest threat" to American birds and warning that "nearly half" of North America's bird species were at risk of losing their habitats by 2080. Audubon's announcement was credulously retransmitted by national and local media, including the Minneapolis *Star Tribune*, whose blogger on bird-related subjects, Jim Williams, drew the inevitable inference: Why argue about stadium glass when the *real* threat to birds was climate change? In comparison, Williams said, a few thousand bird deaths would be "nothing."

I was in Santa Cruz, California, and already not in a good mood. The day I saw the Williams quote was the two hundred and fifty-fourth of a year in which, so far, sixteen had qualified as rainy. To the injury of a brutal drought came the daily insult of radio forecasters describing the weather as beautiful. It wasn't that I didn't share Williams's anxiety about the future. What upset me was how a dire prophecy like Audubon's could lead to indifference toward birds in the present.

Maybe it's because I was raised as a Protestant and became an environmentalist, but I've long been struck by the spiritual kinship of environmentalism and New England Puritanism. Both belief systems are haunted by the feeling that simply to be human is to be guilty. In the case of environmentalism, the feeling is grounded in scientific fact. Whether it's prehistoric North Americans hunting the mastodon to extinction, Maori wiping out the megafauna of New Zealand, or modern civilization deforesting the planet and emptying the oceans, human beings are universal killers of the natural world. And now climate change has given us an eschatology for reckoning with our guilt: coming soon, some hellishly overheated tomorrow, is Judgment Day. Unless we repent and mend our ways, we'll all be sinners in the hands of an angry Earth.

I'm still susceptible to this sort of puritanism. Rarely do I board an airplane or drive to the grocery store without considering my carbon footprint and feeling guilty about it.* But when I started watching birds, and worrying about their welfare, I became attracted to a countervailing strain of Christianity, inspired by St. Francis of Assisi's example of loving what's concrete and vulnerable and right in front of us. I gave my support to the focused work of the American Bird Conservancy and local Audubon societies. Even the most ominously degraded landscape could make me happy if it had birds in it.

And so I came to feel miserably conflicted about climate change. I accepted its supremacy as the environmental issue of

*This is one of several sentences that I've added to the original *New Yorker* version of this essay (titled "Carbon Capture") for greater clarity or accuracy.

our time, but I felt bullied by its dominance. Not only did it make every grocery-store run a guilt trip; it made me feel selfish for caring more about birds in the present than about people in the future. What were the eagles and the condors killed by wind turbines compared with the impact of rising sea levels on poor nations? What were the endemic cloud-forest birds of the Andes compared with the atmospheric benefits of Andean hydroelectric projects?

A hundred years ago, the National Audubon Society was an activist organization, campaigning against wanton bird slaughter and the harvesting of herons for their feathers, but its spirit has since become gentler. In recent decades, it's been better known for its holiday cards and its plush-toy cardinals and bluebirds, which sing when you squeeze them, than for generating hard science, taking controversial positions, or partnering with groups that do real conservation work. When the organization shifted into apocalypse mode, last September, I wished that it had stuck with plush toys. Love is a better motivator than guilt.

In rolling out its climate-change initiative, Audubon alluded to the "citizen science data" it had mobilized, and to a "report," prepared by its own scientists, that justified its dire predictions. Visitors to its updated website were treated to images of climate-imperiled species, such as the Bald Eagle, and asked to "take the pledge" to help save them. The actions that Audubon suggested to pledge-takers were gentle stuff—tell your stories, create a bird-friendly yard—but the website also offered a "Climate Action Pledge," which was long and detailed and included things like replacing your incandescent lightbulbs with lower-wattage alternatives.

The climate-change report was not immediately available, but from the website's graphics, which included range maps of various bird species, it was possible to deduce that the report's method involved a comparison of a species' present range with its predicted range in a climate-altered future. When there was broad overlap between the two ranges, it was assumed that the species would survive. When there was little or no overlap, it was assumed that the species would be caught between an old range that had grown inhospitable to it and a new range in which the habitat was wrong, and would be at risk of disappearing.

This kind of modeling can be useful, but it's fraught with uncertainties. A species may currently breed in a habitat with a particular average temperature, but this doesn't mean that it couldn't tolerate a higher temperature, or that it couldn't adapt to a slightly different habitat farther north, or that the more northerly habitat won't change as temperatures rise. North American species in general, having contended with blazing July days and frosty September nights as they evolved, are much more tolerant of temperature fluctuations than tropical species are. Although, in any given place, some familiar back-yard birds may have disappeared by 2080, species from farther south are likely to have moved in to take their place. North America's birdlife may well become more diverse, not less.

The Bald Eagle was an especially odd choice of poster bird for Audubon's initiative. The species nearly became extinct fifty years ago, before DDT was banned. The only reason we can worry about its future today is that the public—led by the then energetic Audubon—rallied around an *immediate* threat to it. The eagle's plight was a primary impetus for the Endangered Species Act of 1973, and the eagle is one of the act's great success stories. Once its eggs were no longer weakened by DDT, its population and range expanded so dramatically that it was removed from the endangered-species list in 2007. The eagle rebounded because it's a resilient and resourceful bird, a generalist hunter and scavenger, capable of traveling long distances to colonize new territory. It's hard to think of a species less liable to be trapped by geography. Even if global warming squeezes it entirely out of its current summer and winter ranges, the melting of ice in Alaska and Canada may actually result in a larger new range.

But climate change is seductive to organizations that want to be taken seriously. Besides being a ready-made meme, it's usefully imponderable: while peer-reviewed scientific estimates put the annual American death toll of birds from collisions and from outdoor cats at more than three billion, no individual bird death can be definitively attributed to climate change, still less to any climate action that an ordinary citizen did or didn't take. (Local and short-term weather patterns are the chaotic product of a host of variables, and whether one person drives a Hummer or a Prius has nothing to do with them.) Although you could demonstrably save the lives of the birds now colliding with your windows or being killed by your cats, reducing your carbon footprint even to zero saves nothing. Declaring climate change bad for birds is therefore the opposite of controversial. To demand stricter review of wind farms, to make sure they're not built directly in the path of millions of migrating birds, would alienate environmental groups that favor wind power at any cost. To take an aggressive stand against the overharvesting of horseshoe crabs (the real reason that the Red Knot, a shorebird, had to be put on the list of threatened U.S. species this winter) might embarrass the Obama administration, whose director of the Fish and Wildlife Service, in announcing the listing, laid the blame for the Red Knot's decline primarily on "climate change," a politically more palatable culprit. Climate change is everyone's fault—in other words, no one's. We can all feel good about deploring it.

There's no doubt that the coming century will be a tough one for wild animals. Even if climate scientists are wrong, and global temperatures miraculously stabilize tomorrow, we would still be facing the largest extinction event in sixty-five million years. What remains of the natural world is rapidly being destroyed by our rising population, by deforestation and intensive agriculture, by depletion of fisheries and aquifers, by pesticide and plastic pollution, and by the spread of invasive species. For countless species, including almost all of North America's birds, climate change is a more distant and secondary threat. The responses of birds to acute climatic stress are not well studied, but birds have been adapting to such stresses for tens of millions of years, and they're surprising us all the time—Emperor Penguins relocating their breeding grounds as the Antarctic ice melts, Tundra Swans leaving the water and learning to glean grains from agricultural fields. Not every species will manage to adapt. But the larger and healthier and more diverse our bird populations, the greater the chances that many species will survive, even thrive. To prevent extinctions in the future, it's not enough to curb our carbon emissions. *We also have to keep a whole lot of wild birds alive right now.* We need to combat the extinctions that are threatened in the present, work to reduce the many hazards that are decimating North American bird populations, and invest in large-scale, intelligently conceived conservation efforts, particularly those designed to allow for climate change. These aren't the only things that people who care about nature should be doing. But it only makes sense *not* to do them if the problem of global warming demands the full resources of every single nature-loving group.

A little tragicomedy of climate activism is its shifting of goalposts. Ten years ago, we were told that we had ten years to take the kind of drastic actions needed to prevent global temperatures from rising more than two degrees Celsius in this century. Today we hear, from some of the very same activists, that *we still have ten years*. In reality, our actions now would need to be even more drastic than they would have ten years ago, because further gigatons of carbon have accumulated in the atmosphere. At the rate we're going, we'll use up our entire emissions allowance for the century before we're even halfway through it. Meanwhile, the actions that many governments now propose are *less* drastic than what they proposed ten years ago.

A book that does justice to the full tragedy and weird comedy of climate change is *Reason in a Dark Time*, by the philosopher Dale Jamieson. Ordinarily, I avoid books on the subject, but a friend recommended it to me last summer, and I was intrigued by its subtitle, "Why the Struggle Against Climate Change Failed—and What It Means for Our Future." I was intrigued by the word *failed* in particular, the past tense of it. I started reading and couldn't stop.

Jamieson, an observer and participant at climate conferences since the early nineties, begins with an overview of humanity's response to the largest collective-action problem it has ever faced. In the twenty-three years since the Rio Earth Summit, at which hopes for a global agreement ran high, not only have carbon emissions not decreased; they've increased steeply. In Copenhagen, in 2009, President Obama was merely ratifying a fait accompli when he declined to commit the United States to binding targets for reductions. Unlike Bill Clinton, Obama was frank about how much action the American political system could deliver on climate change: none. Without the United States, which is the world's second-largest emitter of greenhouse gases, a global agreement isn't global, and other countries have little incentive to sign it. Basically, America has veto power, and we've exercised it again and again.

The reason the American political system can't deliver action isn't simply that fossil-fuel corporations sponsor denialists and buy elections, as many progressives suppose. Even for people who accept the fact of global warming, the problem can be framed in many different ways—a crisis in global governance, a market failure, a technological challenge, a matter of social justice, and so on—each of which argues for a different expensive solution. A problem like this (a "wicked problem" is the technical term) will frustrate almost any country, and it's particularly difficult to solve in the United States, where government is designed to be both weak and responsive to its citizens. Unlike the progressives who see a democracy perverted by moneyed interests, Jamieson suggests that America's inaction on climate change is the *result* of democracy. A good democracy, after all, acts in the interests of its citizens, and it's precisely the citizens of the major carbon-emitting democracies who benefit from cheap gasoline and global trade, while the main costs of our polluting are borne by those who have no vote: poorer countries, future generations, other species. The American electorate, in other words, is rationally self-interested. According to a survey cited by Jamieson, more than sixty percent of Americans believe that climate change will harm other species and future generations, while only thirty-two percent believe that it will harm them personally.

Shouldn't our responsibility to other people, both living and not yet born, compel us to take radical action on climate change? The problem here is that it makes no difference to the climate whether any individual, myself included, drives to work or rides a bike. The scale of greenhouse-gas emissions is so vast, the mechanisms by which these emissions affect the climate so non-linear, and the effects so widely dispersed in time and space, that no specific instance of harm could ever be traced back to my 0.0000001% contribution to emissions. I may abstractly fault myself for emitting way more than the global per capita average. But if I calculate the average annual carbon quota required to limit global warming to two degrees this century, I find that simply maintaining a typical American single-family home exceeds it in two weeks. Absent any indication of direct harm, what makes intuitive moral sense is to live the life I was given, be a good citizen, be kind to the people near me, and conserve as well as I reasonably can.

Jamieson's larger contention is that climate change is different in category from any other problem the world has ever faced. For one thing, it deeply confuses the human brain, which evolved to focus on the present, not the far future, and on readily perceivable movements, not slow and probabilistic developments. (When Jamieson notes that "against the background of a warming world, a winter that would not have been seen as anomalous in the past is viewed as unusually cold, thus as evidence that a warming is not occurring," you don't know whether to laugh or to cry for our brains.) The great hope of the Enlightenment—that human rationality would enable us to transcend our evolutionary limitations—has taken a beating from wars and genocides, but only now, on the problem of climate change, has it foundered altogether.

I'd expected to be depressed by *Reason in a Dark Time*, but I wasn't. Part of what's mesmerizing about climate change is its vastness across both space and time. Jamieson, by elucidating our past failures and casting doubt on whether we'll ever do any better, situates it within a humanely scaled context. "We are constantly told that we stand at a unique moment in human history and that this is the last chance to make a difference," he writes in his introduction. "But every point in human history is unique, and it is always the last chance to make some particular difference."

This was the context in which the word *nothing*, applied to the particular difference that some Minnesotan bird lovers were trying to make, so upset me. It's not that we shouldn't care whether global temperatures rise two degrees or six this century, or whether the oceans rise twenty inches or twenty feet; the differences matter immensely. Nor should we fault any promising effort, by foundations or NGOs or governments, to mitigate global warming or adapt to it. The question is whether everyone who cares about the environment is obliged to make climate the overriding priority. Does it make any practical or moral sense, when the lives and the livelihoods of millions of people are at risk, to care about a few thousand warblers colliding with a stadium?

To answer the question, it's important to acknowledge that drastic planetary overheating is a done deal. Even in the nations most threatened by flooding or drought, even in the countries most virtuously committed to alternative energy sources, no head of state has ever made a commitment to leaving any carbon in the ground. Without such a commitment, "alternative" merely means "additional"—postponement of human catastrophe, not prevention. The Earth as we now know it resembles a patient with bad cancer. We can choose to treat it with disfiguring aggression, damming every river and blighting every landscape with biofuel agriculture, solar farms, and wind turbines, to buy some extra years of moderated warming. Or we can adopt a course of treatment that permits a higher quality of life, still fighting the disease but protecting the areas where wild animals and plants are hanging on, at the cost of slightly hastening the human catastrophe. One advantage of the latter approach is that, if a miracle cure like fusion energy should come along, or if global consumption rates and population should ever decline, there might still be some intact ecosystems to save.

Choosing to preserve nature at potential human expense would be morally more unsettling if nature still had the upper hand. But we live in the Anthropocene—in a world ever more of our own making. Near the end of Jamieson's chapter on ethics, he poses the question of whether it's a good thing or a bad thing that the arcadian Manhattan of 1630, lushly forested and teeming with fish and birds, became the modern Manhattan of the High Line and the Metropolitan Museum. Different people will give different answers. The point is that the change occurred and can't be undone, as global warming can't be undone. We were bequeathed a world of goods and bads by our forebears, and we'll bequeath a world of different goods and bads to our descendants. We've always been not only universal despoilers but brilliant adapters; climate change is just the same old story writ larger. The only self-inflicted existential threats to our species are nuclear war and genetically modified microorganisms.

The story that is genuinely new is that we're causing mass extinctions. Not everyone cares about wild animals, but the people who consider them an irreplaceable, non-monetizable good have a positive ethical argument to make on their behalf. It's the same argument that Rachel Carson made in *Silent Spring*, the book that ignited the modern environmental movement. Carson did warn of the dangers of pollution to human beings, but the moral center of her book was implicit in its title: Are we really okay with eliminating birds from the world? The dangers of carbon pollution today are far greater than those of DDT, and climate change may indeed be, as the National Audubon Society says, the foremost long-term threat to birds. But I already know that we can't prevent global warming by changing our lightbulbs. I still want to do *something*.

In *Annie Hall*, when the young Alvy Singer stopped doing his homework, his mother took him to a psychiatrist. It turned out that Alvy had read that the universe is expanding, which would surely lead to its breaking apart someday, and to him this was an argument for not doing his homework: "What's the point?" Under the shadow of vast global problems and vast global remedies, smaller-scale actions on behalf of nature can seem similarly meaningless. But Alvy's mother was having none of it. "You're here in Brooklyn!" she said. "Brooklyn is not expanding!" It all depends on what we mean by meaning.

Climate change shares many attributes of the economic system that's accelerating it. Like capitalism, it is transnational, unpredictably disruptive, self-compounding, and inescapable. It defies individual resistance, creates big winners and big losers, and tends toward global monoculture—the extinction of difference at the species level, a monoculture of agenda at the institutional level. It also meshes nicely with the tech industry, by fostering the idea that only tech, whether through the efficiencies of Uber or some masterstroke of geoengineering, can solve the problem of greenhouse-gas emissions. As a narrative, climate change is almost as simple as "Markets are efficient." The story can be told in fewer than a hundred and forty characters: We're taking carbon that used to be sequestered and putting it in the atmosphere, and unless we stop we're fucked.

Conservation work, in contrast, is novelistic. No two places are alike, and no narrative is simple. When I traveled to Peru last November to see the work of a Peruvian-American partnership, the Amazon Conservation Association, my first stop was at a small indigenous community in the highlands east of Cuzco. With Amazon Conservation's help, the community is reforesting Andean slopes, suppressing forest fires, and developing a business in a local legume called tarwi, which can thrive on degraded land and is popular enough in Cuzco to be profitable. In an old and dusty and dirt-floored building, women from the community served me a lunch of tarwi stew and dense, sweet tarwi bread. After lunch, in a neighboring courtyard, I toured a nursery of native tree saplings that the community will hand-plant on steep slopes, to fight erosion and improve local water quality. I then visited a nearby community that has pledged to leave its forested land intact and is operating an experimental organic farm. The scale of the farm is small, but to the community it means clear streams and self-sustenance, and to Amazon Conservation it represents a model for other communities. The regional and municipal governments have money from petroleum and mining royalties, and could spend it revitalizing the highlands according to the model. "We're not jealous," Amazon Conservation's Peruvian director, Daniela Pogliani, told me. "If the government wants to take our ideas and take the credit, we have no problem with it."

In an era of globalism of every sort, a good conservation project has to meet new criteria. The project has to be *large*, because biodiversity won't survive in a habitat fragmented by palm-oil plantations or gas drilling. The project also has to respect and accommodate the people already living in and around it. (Carbon emissions have rendered meaningless the ideal of a wilderness untouched by man; the new ideal is "wildness," which is measured not by isolation from disturbance but by the diversity of organisms that can complete their life cycles.) And the project needs to be resilient with respect to climate change, either by virtue of its size or by incorporating altitudinal gradients or multiple microclimates.

The highlands are important to the Amazon because they're a source of its water and because, as the planet heats up, lower-elevation species will shift their ranges upslope. The focal point for Amazon Conservation is Peru's Manú National Park, a swath of lower-elevation rain forest larger than Connecticut. The park, which is home to indigenous groups that shun contact with the outside world, has full legal protection from encroachment, but illegal encroachment is endemic in the parks of tropical countries. What Amazon Conservation is attempting to do for Manú, besides expanding its upslope potential and protecting its watershed, is to strengthen the buffer on the flanks of the park, which are threatened by logging, slash-and-burn farming, and a boom in wildcat gold mining in the region of Madre de Dios. Even if it were politically feasible for Amazon Conservation, a half-American NGO, to simply buy up all the land, it couldn't afford to do it. The project aspires, instead, to be a protective belt of small reserves, self-sustaining community lands, and larger conservation "concessions" on state-owned land.

On the fifty-five-mile road down from the highlands, it's possible to see nearly six hundred bird species. The road follows an ancient track once used to transport coca leaves from the lowlands to pre-Columbian highland civilizations. On trails near the road, Amazon Conservation researchers peaceably coexist with modern-day coca traffickers. The road bottoms out near Villa Carmen, a former hacienda that now has an educational center, a lodge for ecotourists, and an experimental farm where a substance called biochar is being tested. Biochar, which is manufactured by kiln-burning woody refuse and pulverizing the charred result, allows carbon to be sequestered in farm fields and is a low-cost way to enrich poor soil. It offers local farmers an alternative to slash-and-burn agriculture, wherein forest is destroyed for cropland, the soil is quickly exhausted, and more forest has to be destroyed. Even a wealthy country like Norway, seeking to offset its carbon emissions and to assuage its guilt, can't save a rain forest simply by buying up land and putting a fence around it, because no fence is strong enough to resist social forces. The way to save a forest is to give the people who live in it alternatives to cutting it down.

At the indigenous village of Santa Rosa de Huacaria, near Villa Carmen, the community's cacique, Don Alberto Manqueriapa, gave me a tour of the fish farm and fish hatchery that Amazon Conservation has helped it develop. Large-scale fish farming is ecologically problematic in other parts of the world, but smaller-scale operations in the Amazon, using native fish species, such as pacu, are among the most sustainable and least destructive sources of animal protein. Huacaria's operation provides meat for its thirty-nine families and surplus fish that it can sell for cash. Over lunch—farmed pacu fire-roasted with yuca inside segments of bamboo, with heliconia-leaf plugs at each end—Don Alberto held forth movingly on the effects of climate change that he'd seen in his lifetime. The sun felt hotter now, he said. Some of his people had developed skin cancer, unheard of in the past. Nevertheless, he was committed to the forest. Amazon Conservation is helping the community expand its land title and develop its own partnership with the national park. Don Alberto told me that a natural-medicine company had offered him a retainer and a jet in which to fly around the world and lecture on traditional healing, and that he'd turned it down.

The most striking thing about Amazon Conservation's work is the smallness of its constituent parts. There are the eight female pacu from which a season's worth of eggs are taken, the humbleness of the plastic tanks in which the hatchlings live. There are the conical piles of dirt that highland women sit beside and fill little plastic bags in which to plant tree seedlings. There are the simple wooden sheds that Amazon Conservation builds for indigenous Brazil-nut harvesters to shelter the nuts from rain, and that can make the difference between earning a living income and having to cut or leave the forest. And there is the method for taking a bird census in the lowlands: you walk a hundred meters, stopping to look and listen, and then walk another hundred meters. At every turn, the smallness contrasts with the vastness of climate-change projects—the mammoth wind turbines, the horizon-reaching solar farms, the globe-encircling clouds of reflective particles that geoengineers envision. The difference in scale creates a difference in the kind of meaning that actions have for the people performing them. The meaning of climate-related actions, because they produce no discernible result, is necessarily eschatological; they refer to a Judgment Day we're hoping to postpone. The mode of meaning of conservation in the Amazon is Franciscan: you're helping something you love, something right in front of you, and you can see the results.

In much the way that developed nations, having long contributed disproportionately to carbon emissions, now expect developing nations to share the burden of reducing them, the rich but biotically poor countries of Europe and North America need tropical countries to do the work of safeguarding global biodiversity. Many of these countries are still recovering from colonialism, however, and have more urgent troubles. Very little of the deforestation of the Brazilian Amazon, for example, is being done by wealthy people. The deforesters are poor families displaced from more fecund regions where capital-intensive agribusinesses grow sugarcane, for ethanol and soft drinks, and eucalyptus that is pulped for American disposable diapers. The gold-mining boom in Madre de Dios is not only an ecological catastrophe but a human disaster, with widespread reports of mercury poisoning and human trafficking, but Peruvian state and federal governments have yet to put an end to it, because the miners make much better money than they could in the impoverished regions from which they've emigrated. Besides tailoring its work to the needs and capacities of local people, a group like Amazon Conservation has to negotiate an extremely complicated political landscape.

In Costa Rica, I met a seventy-six-year-old tropical biologist, Daniel Janzen, who has spent nearly half his life doing just that. Janzen and his wife, Winnie Hallwachs, are the architects of perhaps the most audacious and successful conservation project in the New World tropics, the Área de Conservación Guanacaste (ACG). Janzen and Hallwachs began working on the project, in 1985, with many advantages. Costa Rica was a stable democracy whose system of parks and reserves comprised one-quarter of its land area and was internationally admired, and the northern dry-forest region of Guanacaste, the site of the project, was remote, sparsely populated, and unattractive to agribusiness. That Janzen and Hallwachs created a reserve that meets the new criteria—it is huge, has good relations with surrounding communities, and encompasses a marine reserve, the dry slopes of a volcanic cordillera, and Caribbean rain forest—is nonetheless remarkable, because they were two unwealthy scientists and the politics never ceased to be complicated.

Costa Rica famously has no army, but its park administration has been organized like one. Headquartered in the capital, San José, it freely rotates its guards and other personnel throughout the system, with the parks functioning essentially as territories to be defended from armies of potential encroachers. Janzen and some farsighted Costa Rican policymakers recognized that, in a country where economic opportunities were limited, the amount of protected land enormous, and funding for protection strictly finite, defending parks filled with timber and game and minerals was like defending mansions in a ghetto. The ACG experimented with a new approach: the national parks and the reserves within it were exempted from the park administration's policy of rotation, which allowed their personnel to put down roots and develop allegiance to the land and to the conservation concept, and all employees, including the police, were expected to do meaningful conservation or scientific work.

In the early years, this work often consisted of fighting fires. Much of the present-day ACG was once ranchland covered with Africanized grasses. Using money raised with the help of the Nature Conservancy and the Swedish and Costa Rican governments, and from passing a hat after his lectures in America, Janzen was able to buy up huge chunks of pasture and damaged forest between the two existing national parks. After the cattle were removed, wildfires became the main threat to the project. Janzen experimented with planting seedlings of native tree species, but he quickly concluded that natural reforestation, with seeds carried by wind and animal droppings, worked better. Once the new forest took hold, and the fire risk diminished, he developed a more ambitious mission for the ACG's employees: creating a complete inventory of the estimated 375,000 plant and animal species that occur within its boundaries.

Borrowing from the term *paralegal*, Janzen coined the word *parataxonomist* for the Guanacasteans he hired. They lack university degrees, but after a period of intensive training they're able to do real scientific work. They walk the dry Pacific-slope forest and the wet Caribbean forest, collect specimens, and mount them and take tissue samples for DNA analysis. There are currently thirty-four parataxonomists, whom Janzen is able to pay respectable salaries with grant money, interest from a small endowment, and dogged fund-raising. Janzen told me that the parataxonomists are as highly motivated and eager to learn as his best graduate students. (He teaches biology at the University of Pennsylvania.) I saw one team early on a Saturday morning collecting an assortment of leaves for the caterpillars it was raising in plastic bags, another team setting out on a Sunday morning to scour the woods for specimens.

Of the three new criteria for successful conservation projects, integration with surrounding communities is the most difficult to meet. Janzen's taxonomy endeavor serves this goal in several ways. Most basically, for Costa Ricans to care about biodiversity—their country, which covers 0.03 percent of the Earth's land surface, contains four percent of its species—they have to know what it consists of. Biodiversity is an abstraction, but the hundreds of drawers of pinned and named Guanacastean moth specimens, in an air-conditioned room at Santa Rosa National Park, are not. Hands-on science, the specific story that each toxic plant and each parasitic wasp has to tell, also provides a focus for the Guanacastean schoolchildren whom the ACG has been hosting for thirty years. If you spent a week in the dry forest as a child, examining chrysalides and ocelot droppings, you might, as an adult, see the forest as something other than a purely economic resource.

Finally, and perhaps most important, the parataxonomists create a sense of local ownership. Some of them are husband-and-wife teams, and many live at the research stations that dot the ACG, where they exert a more powerful protective influence than armed guards ever could, because their neighbors are their friends and family. During my days at Guanacaste, I passed the station at the entrance to Santa Rosa many times and never saw a guard. By Janzen's account, poaching and illegal logging are much rarer in the ACG than in other, traditionally guarded Costa Rican parks.

Janzen and Hallwachs spend half the year in a tiny, cluttered hut near Santa Rosa's headquarters. Deer, agoutis, magpie-jays, wasps, and monkeys frequent the bowls of water in front of their hut. Over the years, they've kept a porcupine and a pygmy owl as rescue pets; Janzen remarked to me wistfully that he wished it were possible to have a pet rattlesnake. White-bearded and shirtless, wearing only sneakers and dirty green cotton pants, he looks as if he'd walked out of a Conrad novel. Hallwachs, who is a tropical ecologist, is younger, more emollient, and skilled at converting Janzen's scientific rationality into conventional social currency.

The forest in Santa Rosa seemed desperately dry to me, even for a dry forest in the dry season. Hallwachs pointed to the cloud cover on the volcanoes and said that during the past fifteen years it has steadily moved upslope, a harbinger of climate change. "I used to win cases of beer betting on the date the rains would come," Janzen said. "It was always May fifteenth, and now you don't know when they're going to come." He added that insect populations in Guanacaste had collapsed in the four decades he'd been studying them, and that he'd thought of describing the collapse in a paper, but what would be the point? It would only depress people. The loss of insect species is already harming the birds that eat them and the plants that need pollination, and the losses will surely continue as the planet warms. But to Janzen the warming doesn't obviate the ACG. "If you had the only Rembrandt in the world," he said, "and somebody came and slashed it with a knife—would you throw it away?"

My visit coincided with the news of a breakthrough in technology for making ethanol from cellulose. From a climate perspective, the lure of efficient biofuel production is irresistible, but to Janzen it looks like another disaster. The richest land in Costa Rica is already given over to monocultural agribusiness. What would happen to the country if second-growth forest could fuel its cars? As long as mitigating climate change trumps all other environmental concerns, no landscape on Earth is safe. Like globalism, climatism alienates. Americans today live far from the ecological damage that their consumption habits cause, and even if future consumers are more enlightened about carbon footprints, and fill their tanks with certified green fuel, they'll still be alienated. Only an appreciation of nature as a collection of specific threatened habitats, rather than as an abstract thing that is "dying," can avert the complete denaturing of the world.

Guanacaste is already the last significant expanse of Pacific dry forest in Central America. To preserve even some of the species unique to it, the reserve has to last forever. "It's like terrorism," Janzen said. "We have to succeed every day, the terrorists have to succeed only once." The questions that he and Hallwachs ask about the future have little to do with global warming. They wonder how to make the ACG financially self-sustaining, and how to root its mission permanently in Costa Rican society, and how to ensure that its water resources aren't all drawn off to irrigate cropland, and how to prepare for future Costa Rican politicians who want to level it for cellulosic ethanol.

The question that most foreign visitors to Guanacaste ask is how its model can be applied to other centers of biodiversity in the tropics. The answer is that it can't be. Our economic system encourages monocultural thinking: there exists an optimal solution, a best conservation product, and once we identify it we can scale it up and sell it universally. As the contrast between Amazon Conservation and the ACG suggests, preserving biological diversity requires a corresponding diversity of approach. Good programs—the Carr Foundation's Gorongosa Restoration Project in Mozambique, Island Conservation's rewilding of islands in the Pacific and the Caribbean, WildEarth Guardians' fight to save the sagelands of the American West, EuroNatur's blending of cultural and biological conservation in southeastern Europe, to name a few—not only act locally but, by necessity, think locally as well.

During my time with Janzen, he rarely mentioned other projects. What concerns him is what he loves concretely: the specific dry-forest hunting grounds that he uses as a tropical field biologist, the unprivileged Costa Ricans who work for the ACG and live near its borders. Sitting in a chair outside his forest hut, he was an unstoppable font of story. There was the story of Oliver North's airstrip for the *contras*, on the Santa Elena peninsula, and how Santa Elena became part of the ACG. The story of Janzen's discovery that dry-forest moth species spend part of their life cycle in humid forest, and how this led him and Hallwachs to expand the scope of their already ambitious project. And the story of the thousand truckloads of orange peel that the ACG took off the hands of an orange-juice plant and agreed to dispose of, in exchange for fourteen hundred hectares of prime forest, and how a mischief-making environmentalist then sued the juice company for illegally dumping the peels on public land, even though, by the time the suit was settled, they'd decayed into a rich, reforestation-promoting loam. The story of how Janzen and Hallwachs learned to do business with multiple landowners simultaneously, making all-or-nothing offers for bundles of properties, to avoid being taken hostage by an individual holdout. The story of the landowner who invested the proceeds of his sale of ranchland in irrigation for sugarcane production outside the ACG—an example of conservation's reversal of geographical entropy, its sorting of mixed-used land into areas of stringent protection and intensive exploitation. And the story of the ACG's redesignation of its schoolteachers as "secretaries," because "schoolteacher" wasn't a recognized civil-service position.

In 1985, when Janzen and Hallwachs set out to create the ACG, with no training or experience in conservation work, they couldn't have imagined any of these stories. Guanacaste became the thing that happened to them, the life they chose to live. It may be true, of course, that "where there's life there's death," as Janzen is fond of saying, and I did wonder if the vision of a climate-denatured planet, a world of switchgrass fields and eucalyptus plantations, is secretly appealing to human beings, because, having so much less life in it, it would have so much less death. Certainly there was death all around me in the forest, palpably more death than in a suburb or a farm field—jaguars killing deer, deer killing saplings, wasps killing caterpillars, boas killing birds, and birds killing everything imaginable, according to their specialty. But this was because it was a living forest.

From a global perspective, it can seem that the future holds not only my own death but a second, larger death of the familiar world. Across the river from the lowest-lying of Amazon Conservation's research stations, Los Amigos, are miles and miles of forest ripped apart by gold miners. The ACG is surrounded by agribusiness and coastal development that its existence has served to concentrate. But within Los Amigos are quetzals, tinamous, trumpeters, and everything else that their ongoing presence represents. Within the ACG is a forest that didn't exist thirty years ago, with hundred-foot trees and five species of large cat, sea turtles digging their nests by the ocean, and flocks of parakeets sociably feasting on the seeds of fruiting trees. The animals may not be able to thank us for allowing them to live, and they certainly wouldn't do the same thing for us if our positions were reversed. But it's we, not they, who need life to have meaning.

CAPITALISM IN HYPERDRIVE

HYPERDRIVE

(*on Sherry Turkle*)

Sherry Turkle is a singular voice in the discourse about technology. She's a skeptic who was once a believer, a clinical psychologist among the industry shills and the literary handwringers, an empiricist among the cherry-picking anecdotalists, a moderate among the extremists, a realist among the fantasists, a humanist but not a Luddite: a grown-up. She holds an endowed chair at MIT and is on close collegial terms with the roboticists and affective-computing engineers who work there. Unlike Jaron Lanier, who bears the stodgy weight of being a Microsoft guy, or Evgeny Morozov, whose perspective is Belarusian, Turkle is a trusted and respected insider. As such, she serves as a kind of conscience for the tech world.

Turkle's book *Alone Together* was a damning report on human relationships in the digital age. By observing people's interactions with robots, and by interviewing them about their computers and phones, she charted the ways in which new technologies render older values obsolete. When we replace human caregivers with robots, or talking with texting, we begin by arguing that the replacements are "better than nothing" but end up considering them "better than anything"—cleaner, less risky, less demanding. Paralleling this shift is a growing preference for the virtual over the real. Robots don't care about people, but Turkle's subjects were shockingly quick to settle for the *feeling* of being cared for, and, similarly, to prefer the *sense* of community that social media deliver, because it comes without the hazards and commitments of a real-world community. In her interviews, again and again, Turkle observed a deep disappointment with human beings, who are flawed and forgetful, needy and unpredictable, in ways that machines are wired not to be.

Her new book, *Reclaiming Conversation*, extends her critique, with less emphasis on robots and more on the dissatisfaction with technology reported by her recent interview subjects. She takes their dissatisfaction as a hopeful sign, and her book is straightforwardly a call to arms: Our rapturous submission to digital technology has led to an atrophying of human capacities like empathy and self-reflection, and the time has come to reassert ourselves, behave like adults, and put technology in its place. As in *Alone Together*, Turkle's argument derives its power from the breadth of her research and the acuity of her psychological insight. The people she interviews have adopted new technologies in pursuit of greater control, only to feel controlled by them. The likably idealized selves that they've created with social media leave their real selves all the more isolated. They communicate incessantly but are afraid of face-to-face conversations; they worry, often nostalgically, that they're missing out on something fundamental.

Conversation is Turkle's organizing principle because so much of what constitutes humanity is threatened when we replace it with electronic communication. Conversation presupposes solitude, for example, because it's in solitude that we learn to think for ourselves and develop a stable sense of self, which is essential for taking other people as they are. (If we're unable to be separated from our smartphones, Turkle says, we consume other people "in bits and pieces; it is as though we use them as spare parts to support our fragile selves.") Through the conversational attention of parents, children acquire a sense of enduring connectedness and a habit of talking about their feelings, rather than simply acting on them. (Turkle believes that regular family conversations help "inoculate" children against bullying.) When you speak to someone in person, you're forced to recognize his or her full human reality, which is where empathy begins. (A recent study shows a steep decline in empathy, as measured by standard psychological tests, among college students of the smartphone generation.) And conversation carries the risk of boredom, the condition that smartphones have taught us most to fear, which is also the condition in which patience and imagination are developed.

Turkle examines every aspect of conversation—with the self in solitude, with family and friends, with teachers and romantic partners, with colleagues and clients, with the larger polity—and reports on the electronic erosion of each. Facebook, Tinder, MOOCs, compulsive texting, the tyranny of office email, and slacktivism all come in for paddling. But the most moving and representative section of the book concerns the demise of family conversation. According to Turkle's young interviewees, the vicious circle works like this: "Parents give their children phones. Children can't get their parents' attention away from their phones, so children take refuge in their own devices. Then, parents use their children's absorption with phones as permission to have their own phones out as much as they wish." For Turkle, the onus lies squarely on the parents: "The most realistic way to disrupt this circle is to have parents step up to their responsibilities as mentors." She acknowledges that this can be difficult; that parents feel afraid of falling behind their children technologically; that conversation with young children takes patience and practice; that it's easier to demonstrate parental love by snapping lots of pictures and posting them to Facebook. But, unlike in *Alone Together*, where Turkle was content to diagnose, the tone of *Reclaiming Conversation* is therapeutic and hortatory. She calls on parents to understand what's at stake in family conversations—"the development of trust and self-esteem," "the capacity for empathy, friendship, and intimacy"—and to recognize their own vulnerability to the enchantments of tech. "Accept your vulnerability," she says. "Remove the temptation."

Reclaiming Conversation is best appreciated as a sophisticated self-help book. It makes a compelling case that children develop better, students learn better, and employees perform better when their mentors set good examples and carve out spaces for face-to-face interactions. Less compelling is Turkle's call for collective action. She believes that we can and must design technology "that demands that we use it with greater intention." She writes approvingly of a smartphone interface that, "instead of encouraging us to stay connected as long as possible, would encourage us to disengage." But an interface like this would threaten almost every business model in Silicon Valley, where enormous market capitalizations are predicated on keeping consumers riveted to their devices. Turkle hopes that consumer demand, which has forced the food industry to create healthier products, might eventually force the tech industry to do the same. But the analogy is imperfect. Food companies make money by selling something essential, not by placing targeted advertising in a pork chop or by mining the data that a person provides while eating it. The analogy is also politically unsettling. Since platforms that discourage engagement are less profitable, they would have to charge a premium that only affluent, well-educated consumers of the sort that shop at Whole Foods are likely to pay.

Although *Reclaiming Conversation* touches on the politics of privacy and labor-saving robots, Turkle shies from the more radical implications of her findings. When she notes that Steve Jobs forbade tablets and smartphones at the dinner table and encouraged his family to talk about books and history, or when she cites Mozart, Kafka, and Picasso on the value of undistracted solitude, she's describing the habits of highly effective people. And, indeed, the family that is doing well enough to buy and read her new book may learn to limit its exposure to technology and do even better. But what of the great mass of people too anxious or lonely to resist the lure of tech, too poor or overworked to escape the vicious circles? Matthew Crawford, in *The World Beyond Your Head*, contrasts the world of a "peon" airport lounge— saturated in advertising, filled with mesmerizing screens—with the quiet, ad-free world of a business lounge: "To engage in playful, inventive thinking, and possibly create wealth for oneself during those idle hours spent at an airport, requires silence. But other people's minds, over in the peon lounge (or at the bus stop), can be treated as a resource—a standing reserve of purchasing power." Our digital technologies aren't politically neutral. The young person who cannot or will not be alone, converse with family, go out with friends, attend a lecture, or perform a job without monitoring her smartphone is an emblem of our political economy's leechlike attachment to our very bodies. Digital technology is capitalism in hyperdrive, injecting its logic of consumption and promotion, of monetization and efficiency, into every waking minute.

It's tempting to correlate the rise of "digital democracy" with steeply rising levels of income inequality; to see more than just an irony. But maybe the erosion of humane values is a price that most people are willing to pay for the "costless" convenience of Google, the comforts of Facebook, and the reliable company of iPhones. The appeal of *Reclaiming Conversation* lies in its evocation of a time, not so long ago, when conversation and privacy and nuanced debate weren't boutique luxuries. It's not Turkle's fault that her book can be read as a handbook for the privileged. She's addressing a middle class in which she herself grew up, invoking a depth of human potential that used to be widespread. But the middle, as we know, is disappearing.

MAY YOUR LIFE BE RUINED

I n a bird market in the Mediterranean tourist town of Marsa Matruh, Egypt, I was inspecting cages crowded with wild turtledoves and quail when one of the birdsellers saw something in my face, some unconscious furrowing of my brow, and called out sarcastically: "You Americans feel bad about the birds, but you don't feel bad about dropping bombs on someone's homeland."

I could have answered that it's possible to feel bad about both birds *and* bombs; that two wrongs don't make a right. But it seemed to me that the birdseller was saying something true about the problem of nature conservation in a world of human conflict, something not so easily refuted. He kissed his fingers to suggest how good the birds tasted, and I kept frowning at the cages.

To a visitor from North America, where bird hunting is well regulated and nobody eats songbirds and only naughty farmboys shoot them, the situation in the Mediterranean is appalling. Every year, from one end of it to the other, hundreds of millions of songbirds and larger migrants are killed for food, profit, sport, and general amusement. The killing is substantially indiscriminate, with heavy impact on species already battered by destruction or fragmentation of their breeding habitat. Mediterraneans shoot cranes, storks, and large raptors for which governments to the north have multimillion-euro conservation projects. All across Europe, bird populations are in steep decline, and the slaughter in the Mediterranean is one of the causes.

Italian hunters and poachers are the most notorious; for much of the year, the woods and wetlands of rural Italy crackle with gunfire and snap with songbird traps. The food-loving French continue to eat ortolan buntings illegally, and France's singularly long list of huntable birds includes many struggling species of shorebird. Songbird trapping is still widespread in parts of Spain; Maltese hunters, frustrated by a lack of native quarry, blast migrating raptors out of the sky; Cypriots harvest warblers on an industrial scale and consume them by the plateful, in defiance of the law.

In the European Union, however, there are at least theoretical constraints on the killing of migratory birds. Public opinion in the EU tends to favor conservation, and a variety of nature-protection groups are helping governments enforce the law. (In Sicily, formerly a hot spot for raptor killing, poaching has been all but eliminated, and some of the former poachers have even become birdwatchers.) Where the situation for migrants is *not* improving is in the non-EU Mediterranean. In fact, when I visited Albania and Egypt, I found that it's becoming dramatically worse.

February 2012 brought eastern Europe its coldest weather in fifty years. Geese that normally winter in the Danube Valley flew south to escape it, and some fifty thousand of them descended on the plains of Albania, starving and exhausted. Every one of them was exterminated. Men using shotguns and old Russian Kalashnikovs mowed them down while women and children carried the carcasses into towns for sale to restaurants. Many of the geese had been banded by researchers to the north; one hunter told me he'd seen a band from Greenland. Although nobody in Albania is going hungry, the country has one of the lowest per capita incomes in Europe. The unusual influx of salable geese was literally a windfall for local farmers and villagers.

The easternmost of Europe's migratory flyways passes through the Balkans, and in Albania the Adriatic coastline, which is otherwise forbiddingly mountainous, opens into an extraordinarily rich system of wetlands, lakes, and coastal plains. For millennia, birds making the northward journey from Africa were able to rest and refuel here before struggling on over the Dinaric Alps to their breeding grounds, and to stop here again in the fall before recrossing the Mediterranean.

Under the forty-year Marxist dictatorship of Enver Hoxha, Albania was an exceptionally repressive police state, its landscape dotted with thousands of mushroom-shaped concrete bunkers facing the country's sealed borders. Totalitarianism destroyed the fabric of Albanian society and tradition, and yet this was not a bad time for birds. Hoxha reserved the privileges of hunting and private gun ownership for himself and a few trusted cronies. He had a hunting lodge on the coast and spent a week there every year. (To this day, the national Museum of Natural History displays bird trophies of Hoxha and other members of the politburo.) But a handful of hunters had minimal impact on the millions of migrants passing through, and the country's command-economy backwardness, along with its repellence to foreign beach tourists, ensured that its wealth of coastal habitat remained intact.

Following Hoxha's death, in 1985, the country underwent an uneasy transition to a market economy, including a period of near anarchy during which the country's armories were broken open and the military's guns were seized by ordinary citizens. Even after the rule of law was restored, Albanians kept their guns, and the country remained understandably averse to regulation of all kinds. The economy began to grow, and one of the ways in which a generation of younger men in Tirana expressed their new freedom and prosperity was to buy expensive shotguns, by the thousands, and use them to do what formerly only the elite could do: kill birds.

In Tirana, a few weeks after the big February freeze, I met a young woman who was very unhappy with her husband's new hunting hobby. She told me they'd had a fight about his gun, which he'd had to borrow money to pay for. He kept the gun in their 1986 Mercedes, and she described how she'd once watched him pull over to the side of a road, jump out of the car, and start shooting at little birds on a power line.

"I'd like to understand this," I said.

"You won't!" she said. "We've talked about it, and I don't understand it." But she called her husband on her cell phone and asked him to join us.

"It's become fashionable, and my friends talked me into it," the hunter explained to me, somewhat sheepishly. "I'm not a real hunter—you can't become a hunter at forty. But being a new one, and feeling good about owning a licensed weapon, a very good powerful gun, and never having killed any birds before: it was fun at first. It was like when summer comes and you feel like jumping in the ocean. It was like having the ball at your feet in front of the goal. I would go out on my own and drive up into the hills for an hour. We don't have well-identified protected areas, and I'd shoot whatever I could. It was spontaneous. But it gets less joyful when you think about the animals you're killing."

"Yes, what about that?" I said.

The hunter frowned. "I feel very uncomfortable with the situation. My friends are saying it now, too: 'There are no birds, we walk for hours without seeing any.' It's really scary. At this point, I'd be happy if the government put a stop to all hunting for two years—no, *five* years—to let the birds recover."

There would be precedent for a fiat like this: seven years ago, when coastal drug and human smuggling became a problem, the government simply banned most private boats and yachts. But electoral power in Albania is narrowly balanced between two major political parties, each of which is reluctant to impose potentially unpopular regulation on an issue of minor concern to most voters.

There is, indeed, only one serious bird advocate in Albania, Taulant Bino, who is also the country's only real birdwatcher. Bino is the deputy minister of the environment, and one morning he took me out to Divjaka-Karavasta National Park, the crown jewel of Albanian coastal preserves, a vast area of outstanding beach and wetland habitat. It was mid-March, a time when hunting is banned throughout the country, and when the park (where hunting is prohibited year-round) ought to have been full of wintering and migrating waterfowl and waders. Except for one pond defended by fishermen, however, and one distant island colony of Dalmatian Pelicans—a majestic and threatened species that Albanians are proud of hosting, although Enver Hoxha did use to shoot them—the park was strikingly devoid of birdlife. There weren't even any mallards.

Driving along the beach, we soon saw one reason why: a group of hunters had put out decoys and were shooting cormorants and godwits. The park's manager, who was escorting us, angrily told the hunters to leave, at which point one of them took out a phone and tried to call a friend in the government. "Are you crazy?" the park manager shouted at him. "Do you realize that I'm here with the deputy minister of the environment?"

Bino's ministry has safeguarded, at least on paper, sufficient habitat to sustain healthy populations of migratory and breeding birds. "When conservationists saw that the economic development might hamper the biodiversity," Bino told me, "they thought they'd better expand the network of protected areas before they were threatened with development. But it's difficult to control people who are armed—you also need the police. We closed one area here in 2007, and four hundred hunters showed up, shooting everything. The police came in and confiscated some weapons, but after two days they said to us, 'This is your problem, not ours.'"

Unfortunately, the old Communist joke still applies to forestry officials responsible for the protected areas: the government pretends to pay them, and they pretend to work. As a result, the laws are not enforced—a fact that Italian hunters, limited by EU regulations at home, were quick to recognize and exploit after Hoxha's death. During my week in Albania, I didn't visit a protected area in which there were *not* Italian hunters, even though the hunting season had ended, even in unprotected areas. In every case, the Italians were using illegal high-quality bird-sound playback equipment and shooting as much as they wanted of whatever they wanted.

On a second visit to Karavasta, without Bino, I saw two men in camouflage getting into a boat with guns, obviously hurrying to push off before I could speak to them. An Albanian helper of theirs, standing on the beach, told me that they were Albanians, but when I called out to them they shouted back in Italian.

"Okay, they're Italians," the helper admitted as they motored away from us. "Cardiologists from Bari, very well equipped. They were out here from dawn to midnight yesterday."

"Do they know the hunting season is over?" I asked.

"They're smart men."

"How did they get into the national park?"

"It's an open gate."

"And who gets paid off? The guards?"

"Not the guards. It's higher up."

"The park manager?"

The helper shrugged.

Albania was once ruled by Italy, and many Albanians still view Italians as models of sophistication and modernity. Beyond the very considerable immediate damage that Italian tourist hunters do in Albania, they've introduced both an ethic of indiscriminate slaughter and new methods of accomplishing it—in particular the use of playback, which is catastrophically effective in attracting birds. Even in provincial villages, Albanian hunters now have MP3s of duck calls on their cell phones and iPods. Their new sophistication, coupled with an estimated hundred thousand shotguns (in a country of three million) and a glut of other weapons that can be used opportunistically, has turned Albania into a giant sinkhole for eastern European migratory biomass: millions of birds fly in and very few get out alive.

The smart or lucky ones avoid the country. On a beach in Velipoja, I watched large flocks of ducks fly back and forth in distress, far offshore, further exhausting themselves after crossing the Adriatic, because local hunters in well-spaced beach blinds prevented them from reaching the wetlands where they could feed. Martin Schneider-Jacoby, a bird specialist for the German organization EuroNatur, described to me how flocks of cranes, approaching Albania from the sea, divide in two by age group.

The adult birds continue flying at high altitude while inexperienced first-year birds, seeing attractive habitat below, descend until shots ring out—there's always somebody ready to take potshots—and then rise again and follow the adults. "They're coming from the Sahara," Schneider-Jacoby said, "and they have two-thousand-meter mountains they have to cross. They *need* the rest. They might still have the energy to get over the mountains, but maybe not then for successful breeding."

Across the Albanian border, in Montenegro, Schneider-Jacoby showed me the extensive salt pans at the town of Ulcinj. Until recently, Montenegrin hunters kept the pans as empty of birds as Albania's "protected" areas, just a few miles away, but a nonprofit, the Center for Protection and Research of Birds of Montenegro, has provided for a single ranger to report poachers to the police, and the results have been dramatic: birds as far as the eye can see, thousands of waders, thousands of ducks, all busily feeding. Spring migration, always awe-inspiring, had never seemed to me more so.

"Eurasia cannot afford a sinkhole like Albania," Schneider-Jacoby said. "We're too good at killing these animals, and we still haven't learned in Europe how to have a system that will allow birds to survive. Hunting bans are the only thing that seems to work right now. If they stop the hunting here, they'll have the best habitat in Europe. People will come to Karavasta to see the resting cranes."

The situation in Albania isn't hopeless. Many new hunters seem aware that something has to change; better environmental education and the coming growth of foreign tourism may increase demand for unspoiled natural areas; and bird populations will rebound quickly if the government enforces the law in protected areas. When I took the hobbyist hunter and his wife to Karavasta and showed them the ducks and waders at the one defended pond, the wife cried out with pride and happiness: "We didn't know we had birds like this here!"*

Farther south, hope is harder to come by. As in Albania, history and politics in Egypt militate against conservation. The country is nominally a signatory to several international conventions regulating bird hunting, but long-standing resentment of European colonialism, exacerbated by tensions over Israel and compounded by the conflict between traditional Muslim culture and the destabilizing freedoms of the West, disincline the Egyptian government to abide by them. What's more, the Egyptian revolution of 2011 was specifically a repudiation of Egypt's police. The new president, Mohamed Morsi, can ill afford to enforce regulations overzealously. He presides over a poor (though by no means starving) country of ninety million, into whose national fabric certain key ethnic groups, like the Bedouin, are less than wholly integrated. He has a lot more urgent worries than wildlife.†

In northeastern Africa, unlike in the Balkans, there is also an ancient, rich, and continuous tradition of harvesting migratory birds of all sizes. (The miraculous provision of meat that

---

*Shortly after my visit, her husband sold his gun. Two years later, following the publication of this story in *National Geographic*, with photographs by David Guttenfelder, the Albanian government instituted a two-year nationwide ban on hunting. The ban has since been renewed for another five years. Enforcement remains a problem, however.

†Indeed, Morsi was deposed in July 2013. He has been in prison ever since.

saved the Israelites in the Sinai Desert, in the biblical account, is thought to have been migrating quail.) As long as the practice was pursued by traditional methods—handmade nets and lime sticks, small traps made of reeds, camels for transportation—the impact on Eurasian breeding bird populations was perhaps sustainable. The problem now is that new technology has vastly increased the harvest while the tradition remains in place.

The most hope-confounding cultural disjunction, however, may be this: Egyptian bird hunters make no distinction between catching a fish and catching a bird. (Indeed, in the Nile Delta, they use the same nets for both.) For many Westerners, birds have a charisma, and thus an emotional and even ethical status, that fish do not. In the desert west of Cairo, while sitting in a tent with six young Bedouin bird hunters, I saw a Yellow Wagtail hopping in the sand outside. My reaction was emotional: here was a tiny, confiding, beautifully plumaged animal that had just flown several hundred miles across the desert. The reaction of the hunter next to me was to grab an air rifle and take a shot. For him, when the wagtail fluttered off unharmed, it was as if a fish had got away. For me, it was a rare moment of relief.

The six Bedouin, barely out of their teens, were camped in a sparse grove of acacias, surrounded in all directions by sand roasting in September sun. They patrolled the grove with a shotgun and air rifles, stopping to flush birds from the acacias by clapping their hands and kicking sand. The grove was a magnet for southbound migrants, and every bird that flew in, regardless of its size or species or conservation status, was killed and eaten. For the young men, songbird hunting was an escape from boredom, an excuse to hang out as a group and do guy things. They also had a generator, a computer loaded with B movies, an SLR camera, night-vision goggles, and a Kalashnikov to fire for fun—they were all from well-to-do families.

Their morning's catch, strung on a wire like a large bunch of fish, included turtledoves, golden orioles, and tiny warblers. There's not much meat on a warbler, or even on an oriole, but to prepare for their long autumnal journey the migrants build up stores of fat, which could be seen in yellow lobes on their bellies when the hunters plucked them. Served with spiced rice, they made a rich lunch. Although orioles are reputed, in the Middle East, to be good for male potency (they're "natural Viagra," I was told), I had no use for Viagra and helped myself only to a turtledove.

After lunch, a hunter came into the tent with the wagtail that I'd seen hopping on the sand. It looked even smaller dead than it had alive. "Poor thing," another hunter said, to general laughter. He was joking for a Westerner.

Because Egyptian desert travel is now by truck, rather than camel, practically every decent-size tree or bush, no matter how isolated, can be visited by hunters during the peak fall season. In some areas, golden orioles are a cash crop, sold to middlemen for freezing and resale in the Persian Gulf states. The Bedouin, however, mostly eat what they catch or give it away to friends and neighbors. At prime sites, such as Al Maghrah oasis, where hunters congregate by the dozens, a single hunter can kill more than fifty orioles in one day.

I visited Al Maghrah late in the season, but the oriole decoys (consisting typically of a dead male on a stick) were still attracting good numbers, and the hunters rarely missed with their shotguns. Given how many hunters there were, it seemed quite possible that five thousand orioles were being taken annually at this one location. And given that there are scores of other desert hunting sites, and that the bird is a prized quarry along the Egyptian coast as well, the losses in Egypt represent a significant fraction of the species' European population of two or three million breeding pairs. Enjoyment of a colorful species with a vast summer and winter range is thus being monopolized, every September, by a relatively tiny number of well-fed leisure hunters seeking natural Viagra. And while some of them may be using unlicensed weapons to kill orioles, the rest are breaking no Egyptian laws at all.

At the oasis, I also met a shepherd too poor to own a shotgun. He and his ten-year-old son instead relied on four nets, hung over trees, and they were mostly catching smaller birds like flycatchers, shrikes, and warblers. The son was therefore excited when he managed to corner a male oriole, resplendently gold and black, in a net. He came running back to his father with it— "An oriole!" he shouted proudly—and cut its throat with a knife. Moments later a female oriole flashed close to us, and I wondered if it might be the dead male's distraught mate. The shepherd boy chased it toward a netted palm tree, but the bird avoided the tree at the last second and headed into the open desert, flying southward. The boy ran after it, cursing: "May your life be ruined!"

Most of the Bedouin I spoke to told me that they won't kill resident species, such as hoopoes and laughing doves. Like other Mediterranean hunters, however, they consider all migratory species fair game—as the Albanians like to say, "They're not our birds." While every Egyptian hunter I met admitted that the number of migrants has been declining in recent years, only a few allowed that overharvesting might be a factor. Some hunters blame climate change; an especially popular theory is that the increasing number of electric lights at the coast is frightening the birds away. (In fact, lights are more likely to attract them.) But the decline occasions only regret, not concern. My Cairene desert guide told me that after the Bedouin had hunted the Houbara Bustard to local extinction—contrary to their professed policy of leaving resident birds alone—they were genuinely sorry it was gone. "It's not that they don't care," he said. "But if the bustard comes back here again, they'll hunt it again."

Environmental advocacy and education in Egypt are mostly confined to a few small nongovernmental organizations, such as Nature Conservation Egypt (which provided assistance with this story). European bird-advocacy groups expend significant money and manpower on Malta and in other European hot spots for migratory bird killing, but the problem in Egypt, which is more severe than anywhere in Europe, is largely overlooked. This represents, perhaps, the inverse of "They're not our birds": *They're not our hunters*. But the political and cultural divide between the West and the Middle East is also daunting. The basic message of environmental "education" is, unavoidably, that Egyptians should stop doing what they've always done; and the concerns of a bird-smitten nation like Britain, whose colonization of Egypt is in any case still resented, seem as absurd and meddling as a Royal Society for the Protection of Catfish would seem to rural Mississippians.

Most Egyptian coastal towns have bird markets where a quail can be bought for two dollars, a turtledove for five, an oriole for three, and small birds for pennies. Outside one of these towns, El Daba, I toured the farm of a white-bearded man with a bird-trapping operation so large that, even after the families of his six sons had eaten their fill, he had a surplus to bring to market. Enormous nets were draped over eight tall tamarisk trees and many smaller bushes, encircling a grove of figs and olives; the nets were an inexpensive modern product, available in El Daba for only the past seven years. The sun was very hot, and migrant songbirds were arriving from the nearby coastline, seeking shelter. Repelled by the net on one tree, they simply flew to the next tree, until they found themselves caught. The farmer's grandsons ran inside the nets and grabbed them, and one of his sons tore off their flight feathers and dropped them in a plastic grain sack. In twenty minutes, I saw a Red-backed Shrike, a Collared Flycatcher, a Spotted Flycatcher, a male Golden Oriole, a Chiffchaff, a Blackcap, two Wood Warblers, two Zitting Cisticolas, and many unidentified birds disappear into the sack. By the time we paused in the shade, amid the discarded heads and feathers of cuckoos and hoopoes and a sparrow hawk, the sack was bulging, the oriole crying out inside it.

Based on the farmer's estimates of his daily take, I calculated that, every year between August 25 and September 25, his operation removes six hundred orioles, two hundred and fifty turtledoves, two hundred hoopoes, and forty-five hundred smaller birds from the air. The supplemental income is surely welcome, but the farm would clearly have thrived without it; the furnishings in the family's spacious guest parlor, where I was treated with great Bedouin hospitality, were brand-new and of high quality.

Everywhere I went along the coast, from Marsa Matruh to Ras el Barr, I saw nets like the farmer's. Even more impressive were the mist nets used for catching quail: ultrafine nylon netting, all but invisible to birds, that is strung on poles and reaches from ground level to eleven or more feet off the ground. The mist nets, too, are a recent innovation, having been introduced in Sinai about fifteen years ago and spread westward until they now cover the entire Egyptian Mediterranean coast. Along the coastal highway west of Sinai, the nets run to the horizon and pass straight through tourist towns, in front of hotels and condominiums.

Much of Egypt's coast is, on paper, protected. But the coastal preserves protect birds only to the extent of requiring permits to erect nets for catching them. These permits are cheap and freely granted; official restrictions on the height and spacing of the nets are honored mainly in the breach. The owners of the nets go out before dawn and wait for quail, arriving from across the sea, to come zinging over the beach and enmesh themselves. On a good day, a third of a mile of nets can yield fifty quail or more. My very low-end estimate, based on figures from a bad year, is that one hundred thousand quail are taken annually in Egypt's coastal mist nets alone.

Even as quail are becoming very difficult to find in much of Europe, the take in Egypt is increasing, due to the burgeoning use of playback technology. The best system, Bird Sound, whose digital chip holds high-quality recordings of a hundred different bird sounds, is illegal to use for hunting purposes in the EU but is nevertheless sold in stores with no questions asked. In Alexandria, I spoke with a sport hunter, Wael Karawia, who claimed to have introduced Bird Sound to Egypt in 2009. Not surprisingly, he'd learned about it from an Italian who hunted in Albania. Karawia said he now feels "very bad, very regretful" about introducing it. Normally, perhaps three-quarters of incoming quail fly over the mist nets, but hunters using Bird Sound can attract the higher-flying ones as well; already all the mist netters in north Sinai are doing it, some of them in spring as well as fall. Hunters on Egypt's large lakes have also begun to use Bird Sound to capture entire flocks of ducks at night.

"It will start to affect the birds, it has to," Karawia told me. "The problem is the mentality—people want to fish anything and hunt anything, with no rules. We already had a lot of guns before the revolution, and since then there's been a forty percent increase. The people who don't have money make their own guns, which is very dangerous—it could get them three years in jail—but they don't care. Even the kids are doing it. School starts in September, but the kids don't start until the hunting season ends."

On the beach in the tourist town of Baltim, I had an encounter with some of these kids. Quail are the only permissible target of mist netters, but there is always a bycatch of small birds and the falcons that prey on them. At sundown in Baltim, walking with a guide from Nature Conservation Egypt and an official from the local protected area, I noticed a beautiful and tiny shorebird, a Little Ringed Plover, caught in a net in the shadow of condominiums. My guide, Wael Shohdi, began to extricate it delicately but stopped when a young man came running up, carrying a mesh bag and trailed by two teenage friends. "Don't touch the bird," he shouted angrily. "Those are our nets!"

"It's okay," Shohdi assured him. "We handle birds all the time."

A tussle ensued as the young hunter tried to show Shohdi how to yank the bird out without damaging the net. Shohdi, whose priority was the safety of the bird, somehow managed to free the plover in one piece. But the hunter then demanded that Shohdi hand it over.

The government official, Hani Mansour Bishara, pointed out that, along with two live quail, the hunter had a live songbird in his bag.

"No, that's a quail," the hunter said.

"No, it's not."

"Okay, it's a wheatear. But I'm twenty years old and we're living from this net."

Not being an Arab speaker, I learned only afterward what they were saying. What I could see in the moment was Shohdi continuing to hold the plover in his hand while the hunter reached for it angrily, trying to grab it away. We were in a country where millions of birds were being killed, but I couldn't help worrying about this individual plover's fate. I urged Shohdi to remind the hunter that it was illegal to keep anything but quail from the nets.

Shohdi did this, but the law was apparently not a good argument to use on an angry twenty-year-old. Instead, with a view to changing hearts and minds, Shohdi and Bishara made the case that the Little Ringed Plover is an important species, found only on mudflats, and that, moreover, it might be carrying a dangerous disease. ("We were lying a little bit," Shohdi told me later.)

"So which is it?" the hunter demanded. "A diseased bird or an important species?"

"Both!" Shohdi and Bishara said.

"If it's true about the disease," one of the teenagers said, "we all would have been dead years ago. We eat everything from the nets—we never let anything go."

"You can still get the disease from cooked birds," Bishara improvised.

My concern about the plover deepened when Shohdi handed it over to the hunter, who (as I learned only subsequently) had sworn by Allah that he would release both it and the wheatear, just not while we were watching.

"But the National Geographic needs to see that they really are released," Shohdi said.

Becoming even angrier, the hunter took out the wheatear and flung it in the air, and then did the same with the plover. Both flew straight to some of their fellows, farther down the beach, without looking back. "I only did it," the hunter said defiantly, "because I'm a man of my word." There wasn't much more than one large bite of meat on the two birds put together, but I could see, in the hunter's bitter expression, how much it cost him to let them go. He wanted to keep them even more than I wanted to see them freed.

Before leaving Egypt, I spent some days with Bedouin falcon trappers in the desert. Even by Bedouin standards, falcon trapping is a pursuit for men with a lot of time on their hands. Some have been doing it for twenty years without catching either of the species, Saker Falcon and Peregrine Falcon, that are prized by middlemen catering to ultrawealthy Arab falconers. The Saker is so rare that not more than a dozen or two are captured in any given year, but the size of the jackpot (a good Saker can fetch more than $35,000, a Peregrine more than $15,000) entices hundreds of hunters into the desert for weeks at a time.

Falcon trapping requires the cruel use of many smaller birds. Pigeons are tied to stakes in the sand and left in the sun to attract raptors; doves and quail are outfitted with harnesses bristling with small nylon slipknots in which Sakers and Peregrines can get their feet stuck; and smaller falcons, such as kestrels, have their eyelids sewn shut and a weighted, slipknot-laden decoy attached to one leg. Hunters drive around the desert in their Toyota pickups, visiting the staked pigeons and stopping to hurl the disabled kestrels into the air like footballs, in the hope of attracting a Saker or a Peregrine—a blinded, weighted kestrel can't fly far. The hunters also often tether an unblinded falcon to the hood of their trucks and keep an eye on it while they speed through the sand. When the falcon looks up, it means that a larger raptor is overhead, and the hunters leap out to deploy their various decoys. The same routine is followed every afternoon, week after week.

One of the two most heartening things I witnessed in Egypt was the rapt attention that falcon hunters gave to my paperback field guide, *Birds of Europe*. They invariably clustered around it and turned its pages slowly, back to front, studying the illustrations of birds they'd seen and birds they hadn't. One afternoon, while watching some of them do this, in a tent where I was offered strong tea and a very late lunch, I was stabbed with the crazy hope that the Bedouin were all, without yet realizing it, passionate birdwatchers.

Before we humans could be served lunch, one of the hunters tried to feed headless warblers to the blinded kestrel and the blinded sparrow hawk that were in the tent with us. The kestrel ate readily, but no amount of pushing the meat into the sparrow hawk's face would induce it to eat. Instead, it busied itself with pecking at the twine that bound its leg—futilely, it seemed to me. But after lunch, when I was outside the tent, letting the hunters try out my binoculars, a sudden shout went up. I turned and saw the sparrow hawk winging purposefully away from the tent and into the desert.

The hunters immediately gave chase in their trucks, in part because the bird was valuable to them but also in part—and this was the other heartening thing I witnessed—because a blinded bird couldn't survive on its own, and they felt bad for it. (At the end of the falcon season, hunters unsuture the eyelids of their decoy falcons and release them, if only because it's a bother to feed the birds year-round.) The hunters drove farther and farther into the desert, worrying about the sparrow hawk, hoping to spot it, but I personally had mixed feelings. I knew that if it got away, and if no other group of hunters happened upon it, it would soon be dead; but in its yearning to escape captivity, even blinded, even at the cost of certain death, it seemed to embody the essence of wild birds and why they matter. Twenty minutes later, when the last of the hunters returned to the tent empty-handed, my thought was: At least this bird had a chance to die free.

A FRIENDSHIP

One afternoon in late summer in 1989, Bill Vollmann called me up and said, "Hey, Jon. Do you like caribou meat? I just came back from the Arctic with some caribou meat that's about to go bad, and Janice is going to make it into a stew." Bill has a speaking voice like no one else's—flat, factual, and hard to read the tone of. Was the implication that I'd eaten enough caribou meat to know if I liked it a subtle joke? What exactly did "about to go bad" mean? With Bill, you never knew.

I was living in Queens at the time, struggling with my second book, and Bill was the first friend I'd made as a published novelist. A year earlier, in Manhattan, my parents and my wife and I had ridden in a hotel elevator with a rumpled middle-aged couple who smiled at me kindly and introduced themselves as Bill's parents. They were in New York for the same literary award ceremony that we were going to. Their son, when I met him at the ceremony, looked more like the winner of a high-school science fair; he had the thick-lensed wireframes, the ill-fitting sport coat, the adolescent complexion, the rough haircut. We'd been talking for no more than two minutes when he proposed, out of nowhere, that we write letters to each other. Neither of us had read the other's work or knew anything about the other, but Bill seemed to have already decided to like me, or was maybe just following one of the bighearted and experience-seeking impulses that are native to him. He caught me off guard with that voice of his.

Only later did I realize that Bill is a dangerous person to try to do anything reciprocal with. When he and I started recommending books to each other, I learned that he not only can read five hundred pages in an afternoon but retains a near-photographic memory of them. After we made a pact to trade our future manuscripts, I got a thick mailer every nine months, while my own next book was so long in coming that I forgot I was supposed to send it to him. In the year after the award ceremony, while I was in Europe, spending my award money, it took me a month to get around to writing him a letter to which he replied the day he got it. He also sent me an advance copy of his new book, *The Rainbow Stories*, and I tore through it—not in an afternoon, but in less than a week—with admiration and amazement. The person I'd met in New York, the nerdy young man with the sweet Midwestern parents, turned out to be a literary genius with intimate firsthand knowledge of the streetwalkers and the skinheads and the winos of mid-eighties San Francisco. The book was the opposite of the cheerful thing its title seemed to promise. Its epigraph was a line of Poe's comparing the varieties of human wretchedness to the hues of the rainbow ("distinct" yet "intimately blended"), and its voice was like Bill's speaking voice, ambiguously poised between limpid sincerity and radical irony. I loved that voice and was now properly flattered that he wanted to be my friend. My wife and I were trying to decide where to go after Europe, and one of the reasons I pushed for New York was that Bill had recently moved there himself.

He and his fiancée, Janice Ryu, had a one-bedroom apartment in a modern high-rise near Sloan Kettering, where Janice was doing her residency in radiation oncology. Her Korean-style preparation of the soon-to-spoil caribou meat, gamey and garlicky, was the first of many dinners I had there. In the summer, I played on my publisher's softball team in Central Park, but in the colder months my only regular exit from married life in Queens was the trips I took on the E or the F train to see Bill. I remember watching *The 400 Blows* on the TV in his bedroom and feeling as if what had been missing from my life was a male writer friend to watch foreign movies with. I'm not sure what I might have imparted to him, besides book recommendations and strongly held opinions, but I learned a lot from him. He showed me the ink drawings that he was making for his books, and I decided to take drawing lessons. He showed me the Mac on which he did all his writing, and I went out and bought my first computer. (But when he complained that he'd developed carpal tunnel syndrome from typing twelve hours every day, all I could do was envy him for his work ethic.) He told me that Janice cut his toenails for him, which was certainly not a service that my own wife was performing. I was pretty sure I didn't want anybody cutting my toenails, but Bill got me thinking that there were all kinds of marriage, not just my own kind. He told me that he liked my wife but that she and I both seemed to be suffocating in the hermetic life we shared. He himself led the least hermetic life imaginable, traveling the world, watching people die, narrowly escaping death himself, and consorting with prostitutes of every nationality. He kept proposing, in his flat-voiced way, that I do journalism or take a trip to some dangerous place.

There, too, I tried to follow his example. I accepted a sexy-sounding assignment in Cincinnati, where the local authorities had recently shut down a show of Robert Mapplethorpe photographs. *Esquire* wanted me to write about the porn outlets and strip clubs of Covington, Kentucky, across the river from

Cincinnati, in order to prove some dubious point about hypocrisy. What would Bill have done? He wouldn't have rested until he'd befriended some strippers, recorded their take on the Mapplethorpe affair, and maybe tried to have sex with one of them. The sex part was beyond my capabilities, but I dutifully went to the strip clubs. They were seedy and depressing and not full of hypocritical Ohioans, and I could sooner have swum back across the river than befriend a stripper. I wrote a flimsy piece of urban sociology and was more relieved than disappointed when *Esquire* killed it, although I could have used the money. It was four years before I tried journalism again.

Bill was born only a few weeks ahead of me, in July 1959, but for a long time I felt far behind him. It's possible that he didn't fully see me for who I am, or that he saw me mainly as a literary project, a younger brother to be encouraged to do the kinds of things he was good at, because those things had worked for him and they might work for me, too. But he was wise, and generous with his wisdom. He could see my situation in my marriage with a clarity that I wouldn't achieve for many years. By the time I caught up with him, and separated from my wife, and became a less timid journalist, he and Janice were living in California again. In the spring of 1996, a week after I'd published a declaration of literary independence in *Harper's*, he came back to Manhattan and invited me to a party at the home of his book editor. After publishing eight books (I'd published two), he was thinking he could use an agent, and he wanted to meet mine. I introduced the two of them at the party, and then, inflated by *Harper's*, I did a Bill-like thing I'd never done before. I went up to a young woman who caught my attention and struck up a conversation with her; I got her number. She and I ended up together for two years, one of them very happy. It was as if Bill had started me down a new road and seen me through to the first station on it. That party was the last time I saw him.

I don't pretend to have read all of Bill's books. He's hyperfertile in the manner of Dickens or Balzac, producing one of those oeuvres that will take people decades to sort out. But, as was already evident in *The Rainbow Stories*, the more appropriate comparison is to Melville and Whitman, writers who, in taking on sprawling new worlds of experience, had few usable literary examples to guide them and so mainly trusted themselves, their own portable instincts and intelligences. Like them, Bill creates forms as he goes. Like them, he's full of an American disdain for authority; he undertakes vast projects; he also produces the occasional clunker. What became his signature form—relatively short passages, arranged by a logic more poetic than narrative and headed with oblique or ironic titles—mirrors his approach to topics that most writers would find too huge to imagine tackling: he atomizes himself and tosses his sensibilities to the wind.

There seems to be nothing that doesn't interest Bill. In "The Blue Yonder," a sublime novella in *The Rainbow Stories*, a character named the Other empties and catalogues the contents of a trash can in Golden Gate Park, looking for clues to the murders of San Francisco winos which he suspects the other side of his split personality is committing. His "autopsy" of the trash can fills two and a half pages:

> . . . three partially squashed Budweiser cans, and a top-sealed Colonel Sanders receptacle for piping hot fryer chickens (now digested, evidently, for what was in there now was a

honey-colored turd).—Below the turd was a blue plastic wrapper for the *New York Times*, a snotty kleenex with the hardened texture of peanut brittle, and a Continental Yogurt cup whose scrapings had separated and partially liquefied and attracted bean-shaped maggots . . .

In a funny footnote, the author attests to having personally explored a trash can on November 13, 1986, and to abbreviating the inventory "so as not to strain your patience." Later in the novella, he attends a pathologist's autopsy of a wino named Evangeline, and his account of this second autopsy runs to eight pages, some of the sentences clinical, some of them lyrical, all of them necessary:

How like a book the body is! We each write our life story in it, describing to perfection what was done to us, what was done by us. Evangeline's liver was a chapter entitled: "What I Wanted." The text was short, but not without pathos. "I wanted to feel loved and warm and happy and dizzy," Evangeline had written. "I wanted to live in the Blue Yonder. I wanted to live in the blue sky and the sun. I wanted to be my own person. I got everything I wanted."—The pathologist went on snipping and snipping.

After *The Rainbow Stories*, my favorite of Bill's books is *The Atlas*. The stories in it are immensely engaged, not just in the physical risks he takes, or in his determination to inject himself into living history, but in his ceaseless quest for meaning and order in a frightening and complicated world. The Atlas who carries the world on his shoulders is essentially the figure of the Artist, as the Romantics and the Moderns conceived of it: the all-assimilating individual subjectivity. And Bill, better than any other American writer now working, is attempting to do for us this heroic work of taking on the entire world. Perhaps it's no surprise, therefore, that the strongest note in *The Atlas*—the almost unbearable overtone to the whole—is the author's loneliness. The moment in the book I can't forget is the night in Berlin when Bill's loneliness becomes so intense that he gives all his money to a prostitute and begs her for a kiss in return. Failing to get one, he approaches three other prostitutes in the street and asks them for a free kiss. One of them obligingly removes a wad of gum from her mouth and then spits in his face: There's your kiss.

Given the richness of Bill's material, it's possible to overlook what a very fine stylist he is. A writer could go to all the places he goes and do all the things he does, and if he didn't also write well none of it would matter. His most willful confusions of fact and imagination, his awfulest catachreses, his most blunt and vulgar factuality all regularly become inspired poetry. What's on the page seems to have come to him as naturally as breathing. As naturally but not as easily. To write like Bill does, there also has to be a passion for the prose, a hunger for beautiful form. One of the things I loved and recognized in him was that he had that passion and he had that hunger. His books have since earned him a cult following for which he's a kind of outlaw hero, an underground adventurer. But those of us who've had the pleasure of his friendship know that when he's talking—as opposed to when he's listening (at which he is a master)—his interests run to grammar and punctuation, to questions like "Who have you been reading?" and "What are her sentences like?"

I'm not sure why Bill and I drifted apart. It may simply be something that happens to writers when they emerge from their respective but still miscible solutions and become more crystalline versions of themselves, or it may be that our particular big-and-little-brother relationship stopped working when I found my new road. There was also the matter of my falling ever farther behind with my reading of Bill's books, and of our no longer sharing a city. He and Janice had settled permanently in Sacramento, and even after I began spending time in Santa Cruz, just three hours away, he was often traveling in some faraway place that he'd found an editor to pay him to report on.

The one time I visited him in Sacramento, in 1995, he took me out to a shooting range and let me fire his .50-caliber Desert Eagle and his Tec-9 semi-automatic. Amid the cordite smoke was a familiar old ambiguity, a whiff of Hemingway flaunting his male prowess (poor Scott Fitzgerald) (but also: poor Hemingway!) intermingled with Bill's boyish enthusiasm for his guns, his pride in his mastery of them, and his patient, uncondescending instruction of a peer who might otherwise never have experienced the kick of a .50-caliber weapon. I felt a little bit one-upped, and I kept getting false-footed by the flatness of his utterances, the deliberate pauses, the almost non-sequiturial way his words come out. But I was happy to be in his presence again. The many chapters of his life were written on his body in the form of a calm, Atlas-like attentiveness and charisma. After we'd fired all his weapons, we went and hung out with Janice in their big suburban-style house, whose petit-bourgeois (Bill's own word for it) decor might have seemed incongruous to someone who knew him only through his outré writing. What I remember best from the house, aside from Bill's huge library, is the framed world map that was hanging in an upstairs hallway. The map was covered with hundreds of pushpins marking all the places Bill had been, many of them remote or dangerous or both. I understood, because I'd had it myself, the impulse to make a map like that, to literally imprint the self on the world, as a way almost of proving that I'd lived and walked the Earth at a particular moment in its history. But looking at Bill's map, in that suburban hallway, I felt—lonely.

Years later, when I was in Santa Cruz and my friend David Wallace had moved to Claremont, Bill called me up with another proposal. "Hey, Jon," he said in his very flattest voice, "have you ever been to the Salton Sea? I'm working on a project down there, and I was thinking maybe you and me and Foster Wallace could get together and go camping." The proposal seemed crazy even by Vollmann standards. The Salton Sea, a dying lake in the desert east of San Diego, is one of the foulest-smelling and least camping-friendly places in the country, and I didn't know anyone who was less of an outdoorsman than David. But I told Bill I'd mention the idea to him. When I did, David responded with a pained silence and changed the subject. Only much later did I see that Bill's proposal had also been brilliant, and regret that I hadn't pressed David harder. Among other things, I'd learned that the Salton Sea is one of the country's premier birdwatching sites, worth suffering its stench and its clouds of flies for. I wished that I could step, for a few days, into an alternate universe in which I camped there with my two gifted friends, a universe in which both of them were still alive and might start their own friendship, because by then, in the universe in which I'm writing this, David was dead and Bill and I had fallen fully out of touch.

A ROOTING INTEREST

(*on Edith Wharton*)

The older I get, the more I'm convinced that a fiction writer's oeuvre is a mirror of the writer's character. It may well be a defect of my own character that my literary tastes are so deeply intertwined with my responses, as a person, to the person of the author—that I persist in disliking the posturing young Steinbeck who wrote *Tortilla Flat* while loving the later Steinbeck who fought back personal and career entropy and produced *East of Eden*, and that I draw what amounts to a moral distinction between the two. But I suspect that sympathy, or its absence, is involved in almost every reader's literary judgments. Without sympathy, whether for the writer or for the fictional characters, a work of fiction has a very hard time mattering.

So what to make of Edith Wharton, on her 150th birthday? There are many good reasons to wish Wharton's work read, or read afresh, at this late literary date. You may be dismayed by the ongoing underrepresentation of women in the American canon, or by the academy's valorization of overt formal experimentation at the expense of more naturalistic fiction. You may lament that Wharton's work is still commonly assumed to be as dated as the hats she wore, or that several generations of high-school graduates know her chiefly through her frosty minor novel *Ethan Frome*. You may feel that, alongside the more familiar genealogies of American fiction (Henry James and the modernists, Mark Twain and the vernacularists, Herman Melville and the postmoderns,

Zora Neale Hurston and the literature of black identity), there is a less noticed line connecting William Dean Howells to F. Scott Fitzgerald and Sinclair Lewis and thence to Jay McInerney and Jane Smiley, and that Wharton is the vital link in it. You may want, as I do, to recelebrate *The House of Mirth*, call much-merited attention to *The Custom of the Country*, and re-evaluate *The Age of Innocence*—her three great like-titled novels. But to consider Wharton and her work is to confront the problem of sympathy.

No major American novelist has led a more privileged life than Wharton did. Although she was seldom entirely free of money worries, she always lived as if she were: pouring her inherited income into houses in rich-person precincts, indulging her passion for gardens and interior decoration, touring Europe endlessly in hired yachts or chauffeured cars, hobnobbing with the powerful and the famous, despising inferior hotels. To be rich like Wharton may be what all of us secretly or not so secretly want, but privilege like hers isn't easy to like; it puts her at a moral disadvantage. And she wasn't privileged like Tolstoy, with his social-reform schemes and his idealization of peasants. She was deeply conservative, opposed to socialism, unions, and woman suffrage, intellectually attracted to the unrelenting worldview of Darwinism, hostile to the rawness and noise and vulgarity of America (by 1914, she'd settled permanently in France, and she visited the United States only once after that, for twelve days), and unwilling to support her friend Teddy Roosevelt when his politics became more populist. She was the kind of lady who fired off a high-toned letter of complaint to the owner of a shop where a clerk had refused to lend her an umbrella. Her biographers, including the estimable R. W. B. Lewis, supply this signal image of the artist at work: writing in bed after breakfast and tossing the completed pages *on the floor*, to be sorted and typed up by her secretary.

Edith Newbold Jones did have one potentially redeeming disadvantage: she wasn't pretty. The man she would have most liked to marry, her friend Walter Berry, a noted connoisseur of female beauty, wasn't the marrying type. After two failed youthful courtships, she settled for an affable dud of modest means, Teddy Wharton. That their ensuing twenty-eight years of marriage were almost entirely sexless was perhaps chiefly a function of her sexual ignorance, the blame for which she laid squarely on her mother. As far as anyone knows, Wharton died having had only one other physical relationship, an affair with an evasive bisexual journalist and serial two-timer, Morton Fullerton. She by then was well into her forties, and the beginner-like idealism and blatancy of her ardor—detailed in a secret diary and in letters preserved by Fullerton—are at once poignant and somewhat embarrassing, as they seem later to have been to Wharton herself.

Her father, a benign but recessive figure, died when she was twenty, after suffering from the financial stresses of providing a luxurious lifestyle for his wife. Wharton, all her life, had only bad things to say about her mother; she also became estranged from both her brothers. She had relatively few friendships with women and none with female writers of her caliber—more strikes against her, in terms of sympathy—but she forged close and lasting friendships with an extraordinary number of successful men, including Henry James, Bernard Berenson, and André Gide. Many were gay or otherwise confirmed in bachelorhood. In the instances where her male friends were married, Wharton seems mostly to have treated the wives with indifference or outright jealousy.

The fine quip of one of Wharton's contemporary reviewers— that she wrote like a masculine Henry James—could also be applied to her social pursuits: she wanted to be with the men and to talk about the things men talked about. The half-affectionate, half-terrified nicknames that James and his circle gave her—the Eagle, the Angel of Devastation—are of a piece with their reports on her. She wasn't charming or easy to be with, but she was immensely energetic, always curious, always interesting, always formidable. She was a doer, an explorer, a bestower, a thinker. When, in her forties, she finally battled free of the deadness of her marriage and became a best-selling author, Teddy responded by spiraling into mental illness and embezzling a good part of her inheritance. She was distraught about this, as anyone would have been, but not so distraught that she didn't force Teddy to pay up; three years later, with firm resolve, she divorced him. Lacking good looks and the feminine charms that might have accompanied them, she eventually became, in every sense but one, the man of her house.

An odd thing about beauty, however, is that its absence tends not to arouse our sympathy as much as other forms of privation do. To the contrary, Edith Wharton's privileges might well seem more forgivable if she'd also looked like Grace Kelly or Jacqueline Kennedy; and nobody was more conscious of the unfair capacity of beauty to override our resentment of privilege than Wharton herself. At the center of each of her three finest novels is a female character of exceptional beauty, chosen deliberately to complicate the problem of sympathy.

The reader of *The House of Mirth* (1905) is introduced to its heroine, Lily Bart, through the gaze of an admiring man, Lawrence Selden, who runs into her by chance at Grand Central station. Selden immediately wonders what Lily is doing there, and he reflects that "it was characteristic of her that she always roused speculation, that her simplest acts seemed the result of far-reaching intentions." To Selden, it's inconceivable that a woman in possession of as much beauty as Lily would not be forever calculating how to use it. And Selden is right about this—Lily, strapped financially, is constantly forced to draw upon her one sure resource—but he is no less wrong. Lily's predicament is that she is never quite able to square those far-reaching intentions with her momentary desires and her tentative moral sensibilities.

On the surface, there would seem to be no reason for a reader to sympathize with Lily. The social height that she's bent on securing is one that she herself acknowledges is dull and sterile, she's profoundly self-involved and incapable of true charity, she pridefully contrasts other women's looks with her own, she has no intellectual life to speak of, she's put off from pursuing her one kindred spirit (Selden) by the modesty of his income, and she's in no danger of ever starving. She is, basically, the worst sort of party girl, and Wharton, in much the same way that she didn't even try to be soft or charming in her personal life, eschews the standard novelistic tricks for warming or softening Lily's image—the book is devoid of pet-the-dog moments. So why is it so hard to stop reading Lily's story?

One big reason is that she doesn't have "enough" money. The particulars of her shortfall may not be sympathetic—she needs to dress well and gamble at bridge tables in order to catch a man who can enable her to dress well and gamble for the rest of her life—but one of the mysterious strengths of the novel as an art form, from Balzac forward, is how readily readers connect with the financial anxieties of fictional characters. When Lily, by taking a long romantic walk with Selden, is ruining her chance to marry the extremely wealthy but comically boring and prudish Percy Gryce, with whom she would have had the bleakest of relationships, you may find yourself wanting to shout at her, "You idiot! Don't do it! Get back to the house and seal the deal with Gryce!" Money, in novels, is such a potent reality principle that the need for it can override even our wish for a character to live happily ever after, and Wharton, throughout the book, applies the principle with characteristic relentlessness, tightening the financial screws on Lily as if the author were in league with nature at its most unforgiving.

What finally undoes Lily, though, isn't the unforgiving world but her own bad decisions, her failures to foresee the seemingly obvious social consequences of her actions. Her propensity for error is a second engine of sympathy. We all know how it feels to be making a mistake, and the deliciousness of watching other people make one—particularly the mistake of marrying the wrong person—is a core appeal of narratives from Oedipus to *Middlemarch*. Wharton compounds the deliciousness in *The House of Mirth* by creating an eminently marriageable heroine whose mistake is to be too afraid of making the mistake of marrying wrong. Again and again, at the crucial moment, Lily blows up her opportunities to trade her beauty for financial security, or at least for a chance at happiness.

I don't know of another novel more preoccupied with female beauty than *The House of Mirth*. That Wharton, who was fluent in German, chose to saddle her lily-like heroine with a beard—in German, *Bart*—points toward the gender inversions that the author engaged in to make her difficult life livable and her private life story writable, as well as toward other forms of inversion, such as giving Lily the looks that she didn't have and denying her the money that she did have. The novel can be read as a sustained effort by Wharton to imagine beauty from the inside and achieve sympathy for it, or, conversely, as a sadistically slow and thorough punishment of the party girl she couldn't be. Beauty in novels tends to cut two ways. On the one hand, we're aware of how often it deforms the moral character of people who possess it; on the other hand, it represents a kind of natural capital, like a tree's perfect fruit, that we're instinctively averse to seeing wasted. Ticking along through the novel, as inexorable as the decline in Lily's funds, is the clock on her youthful good looks. The clock starts running on the very first page—"under her dark hat and veil she regained the girlish smoothness, the purity of tint, that she was beginning to lose after eleven years of late hours and indefatigable dancing"—and it continues to heighten the urgency of Lily's plight, inviting us to share in it emotionally. But only at the book's very end, when Lily finds herself holding another woman's baby and experiencing a host of unfamiliar emotions, does a more powerful sort of urgency crash into view. The financial potential of her youth is revealed to have been an artificial value, in contrast to its authentic value in the natural scheme of human reproduction. What has been simply a series of private misfortunes for Lily suddenly becomes something larger: the tragedy of a New York City social world whose priorities are so divorced from nature that they kill the Darwinianly "fit" woman who ought, by natural right, to thrive. The reader is driven to search for an explanation of the tragedy in Lily's appallingly deforming social upbringing—the kind of upbringing that Wharton herself felt deformed by—and to pity her for it, as, per Aristotle, a tragic protagonist must be pitied.

But sympathy in novels need not be simply a matter of the reader's direct identification with a fictional character. It can also be driven by my admiration of a character who is long on virtues I am short on (the moral courage of Atticus Finch, the limpid goodness of Alyosha Karamazov), or, most interestingly, by my wish to be a character who is *unlike* me in ways I don't admire or even like. One of the perplexities of fiction—and the quality that makes the novel the quintessentially liberal art form—is that we experience sympathy so readily for characters we wouldn't like in real life. Becky Sharp may be a soulless social climber, Tom Ripley may be a sociopath, the Jackal may want to assassinate the French president, Mickey Sabbath may be a disgustingly self-involved old goat, and Raskolnikov may want to get away with murder, but I find myself rooting for each of them. This is sometimes, no doubt, a function of the lure of the forbidden, the guilty pleasure of imagining what it would be like to be unburdened by scruples. In every case, though, the alchemical agent by which fiction transmutes my secret envy or my ordinary dislike of "bad" people into sympathy is *desire*. Apparently, all a novelist has to do is give a character a powerful desire (to rise socially, to get away with murder) and I, as a reader, become helpless not to make that desire my own.

In Wharton's *The Custom of the Country* (1913), as in *The House of Mirth*, an unfit member of old New York society fails to survive. But here the harshly Darwinian "nature" is the new, industrialized, nakedly capitalist America, and the victim is certainly not the protagonist, Undine Spragg. The novel reads like a perfect, deliberate inversion of *The House of Mirth*. It takes the same ingredients of sympathy and applies them to a heroine beside whom Lily Bart is an angel of grace and sensitivity and lovability. Undine Spragg is the spoiled, ignorant, shallow, amoral, and staggeringly selfish product of the economically booming American hinterland; she's named for a hair curler mass-produced by her grandfather. Wharton was working on the novel in precisely the years when she was preparing to forsake the United States permanently, and its grotesquely negative cartoon of the country—the lecherously red face of the millionaire Van Degen, the fatuous pretensions of the celebrity portrait painter Popple, the culpably feeble traditions of old New York, the vacuous pleasure seeking of the arrivistes, the corrupt connivance of business and politics—reads like a selective marshaling of evidence to support her case. The country that can produce and celebrate a creature like Undine Spragg is not, Wharton seems to be arguing to herself, a country she can live in.

But Undine's story is one you absolutely have to read. *The Custom of the Country* is the earliest novel to portray an America I recognize as fully modern, the first fictional rendering of a culture to which the Kardashians, Twitter, and Fox News would come as no surprise. Lewis's *Babbitt* and Fitzgerald's *Gatsby* not only follow directly from it but seem, if anything, somewhat *less* modern. The nexus of money and media and celebrity, which dominates our world today, appears in the novel's opening chapter in the form of the press clippings that Mrs. Heeney (Undine's masseuse and early social adviser) carries with her everywhere, and the clippings become a leitmotif, a recurring measure of Undine's progress. Ignorant though Undine is, she's smart enough to know that she has exactly what reporters need, and she proves remarkably adept at manipulating the press. Along the way, she anticipates two other hallmarks of modern American society: the obliteration of all social distinctions by money, and the hedonic treadmill of materialism. In Undine's world, everything can be bought, and none of it will ever be enough.

The novel's most strikingly modern element, however, is divorce. *The Custom of the Country* is by no means the earliest novel in which marriages are dissolved, but it's the first novel in the Western canon to put serial divorce at its center, and in so doing it sounds the death knell of the "marriage plot" that had invigorated countless narratives in centuries past. The once-high stakes of choosing a spouse are dramatically lowered when every mistake can be—and is, by Undine—undone by divorce. The costs now are mostly financial. And Wharton, who could see the inevitability of her own divorce when she was working on the book, again does nothing by halves. The story is saturated with divorce; it's what the book is relentlessly about. Whereas *The House of Mirth*, a story of irrevocable mistakes, ends with the guttering of the feeble flame of Lily's life, *The Custom of the Country*, which is a story of mistakes without lasting consequences for their maker, ends with the cartoonishly pure spectacle of Undine's marrying the soon-to-be-richest man in America and still not being satisfied. You don't have to admire Undine Spragg to admire an author with the courage and the love of form to go for broke like this. Wharton embraces her new-fashioned divorce plot as zestfully as Nabokov embraces pedophilia in *Lolita*.

Undine is an extreme case of the unlikable person rendered perplexingly sympathetic by her desires. She's almost comically indestructible, like Wile E. Coyote. The interest I take in her ascent—in her Coyote-like survival of the seeming wipe-out blows that her divorces deliver to her social standing—may be akin to the fascination of watching one spider in a jar prevail over other spiders, but I still can't read the book without aligning myself with her struggle. This, in turn, has the odd effect of rendering secondary characters who might be sympathetic (her second and third husbands, her father) less so. I feel annoyed and frustrated with these men for thwarting a progress I've become engrossed in. Their scruples, though admirable in theory, contrast unfavorably with Undine's desires. In this regard, Undine may remind you of Wharton herself, whose success and vitality finally crushed her husband, and whose two great romantic love objects (Berry and Fullerton) it's hard not to think less of, when you read her biography, for not being equal to her love. Undine's sole motivating appetite, which is to have a certain kind of flashy good time, may bear little resemblance to Wharton's sophisticated hunger for art and foreign travel and serious talk, but Undine is nevertheless very much like her creator in being a personally isolated woman doing her best to use what she was given to make her way in the world.

Here, indeed, is a portal to a deeper kind of sympathy for Wharton. Despite all her privileges, despite her strenuous socializing, she remained an isolate and a misfit, which is to say, a born writer. The middle-aged woman tossing her morning pages onto the floor was the same person who, beginning at the age of four, was prone to falling into trancelike states in which she would "make up" stories. She was raised to care about clothes and looks and maintaining proprieties in an elite social milieu, and she spent her twenties and thirties dutifully playing the role for which she'd been bred, but she never stopped being the girl who made up stories. And that girl, perverse, yearning, trapped, is inside all her best novels, straining against the conventions of her privileged world. As if aware of what an unlikable figure she herself cut, she placed unlikable women in the foreground of these novels and then deployed the storyteller's most potent weapon, the contagiousness of fictional desire, to create sympathy for them.

In her most generously realized novel, *The Age of Innocence* (1920), written well after her affair with Fullerton, and after the Great War had made the decades preceding it seem suddenly historical, Wharton told her own story more directly than she ever had before, by splitting herself into a male and a female character, dividing beard from lily. The novel's protagonist, Newland Archer, embodies Wharton's origins: he's an isolated misfit who is nevertheless inextricably enmeshed in the social conventions of old New York and inescapably adapted, despite his yearning not to be, to the comforts and norms of a steady, conservative world. The object of Newland's grand passion, Ellen Olenska, is the person Wharton became: the self-sufficient exile, the survivor of a disastrous and disillusioning marriage, the New York–born European free spirit. They attract each other intensely because they belong together the way two sides of a unitary personality belong together. And so, for once, the problem of sympathy for Wharton's characters isn't a problem at all. There's no making of mistakes here, and money is a minor issue. Ellen is simply pretty and in trouble, and Newland simply wants her but, being married, can't have her.

The beauty of *The Age of Innocence* is that it takes the long view. By setting the main action in the 1870s, Wharton is able, at the end, to bring Newland and Ellen into a radically altered world in which their earlier plight can be seen as the product of a particular time and place. The novel becomes the story not only of what they couldn't have—of what they were denied by the velvet-gloved conspiring of their old New York families—but of what they *have* been able to have. Its great heartbreaking late line, which takes the measure of Newland's unfulfilled desire, is delivered not by Newland or Ellen but by the woman whom Newland has stayed married to. Wharton, in the novel, certainly shines what she once called "the full light of my critical attention" on the social conventions that deformed her own youth, but she also celebrates them. She renders them so clearly and completely that they emerge, in historical hindsight, as what they really are: a social arrangement with advantages as well as disadvantages. In so doing, she denies the modern reader the easy comfort of condemning an antiquated arrangement. What you get instead, at the novel's end, is sympathy.

TEN RULES FOR
THE NOVELIST

1. The reader is a friend, not an adversary, not a spectator.
2. Fiction that isn't an author's personal adventure into the frightening or the unknown isn't worth writing for anything but money.
3. Never use the word *then* as a conjunction—we have *and* for this purpose. Substituting *then* is the lazy or tone-deaf writer's non-solution to the problem of too many *and*s on the page.
4. Write in third person unless a really distinctive first-person voice offers itself irresistibly.
5. When information becomes free and universally accessible, voluminous research for a novel is devalued along with it.
6. The most purely autobiographical fiction requires pure invention. Nobody ever wrote a more autobiographical story than *The Metamorphosis*.
7. You see more sitting still than chasing after.
8. It's doubtful that anyone with an Internet connection at his workplace is writing good fiction.
9. Interesting verbs are seldom very interesting.
10. You have to love before you can be relentless.

MISSING

Maybe it was the sleep medication I'd taken not many hours earlier, or maybe the fifty minutes I'd stood in the security line at JFK, watching JetBlue personnel reward other travelers for their lateness by sending them to the head of the line, but something wasn't right with my head. The time was a quarter after six, and I was standing at the counter of a food station and emptying the very full outer pocket of my knapsack, trying to find a quarter and add it to the six dollars I'd already given the barista for espresso and a muffin. It seemed extremely important to provide exact change—a quarter after six—although I was aware that it was weird of me to think it was important.

Only after I'd located a quarter and loaded my things back into the knapsack did I remember to ask the barista for a receipt, and by then she was ringing up her next customer, a young Latino. I knew I should just forget about expensing my coffee and muffin, but the receipt now seemed extremely important, too. When I asked the barista for a handwritten one, the young Latino offered to give me his own receipt. I thanked him warmly and repaid his kindness by walking away with his rollerboard suitcase.

Ten minutes later, after I'd checked my email and read some football scores, my eyes came to rest on the suitcase at my feet. I'd recently bought a new 21-inch Victorinox rollerboard, and the bag in front of me looked curiously large. It was also not a Victorinox.

I hurried back to the food station and learned that nobody had left a bag there. Recalling that I hadn't put my name and address on my new bag yet, and imagining the ramifications of my mistake—the young Latino had already boarded a plane with my bag! a bag with no personal identification inside or out!—I searched several gate areas and ended up in front of a service counter. There, conferring with a female JetBlue representative, was the young Latino. He was very happy to get his bag back. But he didn't have mine.

"Let's see if we can find it, before we call security," the representative said. "Maybe the gentleman took your bag somewhere without realizing it."

This struck me as unlikely. Someone else must have taken my bag, possibly deliberately; I wondered if I could manage my trip with nothing but my knapsack. As I followed the JetBlue woman back up the concourse, looking at bag after bag attached to its rightful owner, I felt like a birdwatcher who was seeing every imaginable kind of bird except the one kind he was desperate to find. But then we came to another food station, with inferior baked goods, and I remembered that I'd earlier stood at this station and dithered in a cloud of wrongheadedness, looking for a muffin that met my requirements. In front of the muffins, minding its own business, unreported to security in the twenty minutes it had been there, was my Victorinox.

My goal for the trip was straightforward: to see every endemic bird species on two islands, one Greater Antillean and one Lesser, in the seven days I had at my disposal. Species endemic to an island (i.e., found nowhere else on earth) are of special interest to birders who keep lists of the birds they've seen. Endemics that we miss on a particular island are species that we're likely *never* to see, because there are so many other places to go birding before we return to that island, and because, in the Caribbean, many endemics are in trouble and will become only harder to find in the future. If I'd had two weeks, I could reasonably have expected to see every one of Jamaica's twenty-eight and Saint Lucia's four endemics. But to get the job done in a week I would need some good luck.

Although I'm generally not superstitious, I felt as if I'd made a substantial withdrawal from the karma bank by relocating my suitcase at JFK, and I do adhere to the superstition that my luck as a birder is improved by giving generous tips to cabdrivers and hotel staff. So it was a further bad sign that, after I'd been conveyed from the Kingston airport up into the Blue Mountains, I was too slow on the draw to tip the driver.

My host in the mountains, Suzie Burbury, collected me in an SUV and took me up a terrible road to her coffee farm and guesthouse. Until recently, eighty percent of Jamaica's Blue Mountain coffee was exported to Japan, but Japanese demand had crashed since the Fukushima disaster. Jamaica's coffee processors were buying half as much coffee from farmers or halving the price they paid. Suzie and her husband now depended on tourism for income, and more than a third of their guests were birders; the global birdwatching demand for Caribbean endemics is less elastic than the market for coffee.

Suzie gave me quiche and red sorrel iced tea and then sent me out to look for birds. The first endemic I saw, an Orangequit loitering by the road below the farm, was a handsome, gray-blue, orange-throated bird, and I spent some minutes admiring it through my binoculars, but my happiness in seeing it was undeniably bound up in the numbers game that I was playing: one endemic down, twenty-seven to go. I later saw many more Orangequits, and they came to signify little more than "not a species I'm still looking for." It is, of course, a pleasure in itself to walk in a place with abundant and diverse birdlife. It's a way of connecting with a past in which nature was more whole, not fragmented, not degraded—birds being the most visible indicator of a healthy ecosystem. Birding has the added charm and virtue of taking you to parts of a country that most tourists never visit. It makes for a different kind of tourism, in which your First World voyeurism redeems and is redeemed by your obsessive attention to adding species to your life list.

If you hire local bird guides, as I did, you also get to meet people who are hearteningly out of step with their countrymen's indifference or animosity to nature. My guide on my first morning was Lyndon Johnson ("My middle name does not start with B," he told me), a thirty-five-year-old employee of Jamaica's forestry department. After setting out well before dawn, to allow for the badness of the roads, we drove up into high country where tracts of native forest survive amid coffee farms and other development. Within a few hours, Lyndon had found me twelve more endemics. Among them were the Sad Flycatcher, lovely in both name and plumage; the Jamaican Tody, a brilliantly green and gold and red jewel known locally as the Rasta Bird; and the little Arrow-headed Warbler, clad in a black-and-white gabardine vest. The countryside was full of close relatives of this warbler, a dozen different and more colorful North American migrants, whose presence rendered poignant and mysterious the Arrow-headed's insistence on staying rooted to one island while its cousins fly thousands of miles and merely winter in the tropics.

Lyndon also heard, close to the road, one of the country's most elusive endemics, the Jamaican Lizard-Cuckoo, and we stood for a long time and stared into dense forest, hoping for a glimpse. The weather was deliciously unhot, the stillness broken only rarely by trucks carrying groups of coffee-berry pickers. Berries were ripening to red on the slopes below us, which were gouged with mountain-bike trails to which a local entrepreneur had given names like "Ants in the Pants." When it became clear that the cuckoo was in no mood to be seen, we headed to a different forest, closer to Lime Tree, and I had a sense of foreboding about the cuckoo. As in a football game, where you're likewise playing against the clock and an early missed field goal so often comes back to haunt you, early misses of a key endemic can be costly.

By two in the afternoon, when the sun became too hot for the birds to be active, I'd seen eighteen endemics—so many that I'd begun to review them in my mind, consciously connecting each species with the place where I'd seen it. My friend Todd Newberry, author of *The Ardent Birder*, believes that you should list only the species that you can specifically remember encountering: if there's a bird on your list with no memory attached to it, you have to remove it. I personally am not so radical (if my trip list from Ecuador says I saw an Opal-rumped Tanager, then, by God, I must have seen it), but I do believe, with Todd, that birding should be a way of experiencing the place you're in, not just an exercise in making marks on a checklist. The numbers should matter only the way the score of any kind of game matters, as an abstract goal, a way of energizing yourself for an experience that often entails unpleasantnesses—getting up at 4:30 a.m., standing around until your legs ache, being attacked by chiggers or mosquitoes—which you might be inclined to forgo if you didn't have that goal.

That said, I was feeling good about my chances of a sweep: I still had three days and only ten endemics left to find. But it's always a mistake to feel good about your chances. The next morning, when Lyndon and I went walking through beautiful Blue Mountain forest habitat, in perfect cool weather, we found zero new endemics in our first five hours of searching. It was eleven o'clock before Lyndon miraculously spied a black Jamaican Becard in thick foliage that had looked to me devoid of birds. Farther down the road, he spotted a different black bird lurking in a tangle of vines and epiphytes. Although I never saw all of it at once, I was able to piece together its various parts and feel confident that I'd seen a Jamaican Blackbird, the country's rarest endemic. It's found only in undisturbed native forest, which is becoming ever scarcer. I felt bad about its plight but good, in a selfish birdwatcher way, about having added the island's most difficult species to my list. I was now twenty for twenty-eight in just over a day.

At an inn near the northeast corner of the island, I had dinner with my next guide, Ricardo Miller, a government bird specialist and the president of Jamaica's national bird club. Ricardo is handsome, bespectacled, and acute. When he was a boy, growing up in humble circumstances, his ambition was to be a pilot. He joined the Jamaica Combined Cadet Force, and when he was fifteen he secured one of the country's two annual scholarships to train for a pilot's license, on a single-engine Cessna 150. He then applied for the air force and aced the written entrance exam but failed the physical, because he has scoliosis. His plan B was to be a mathematician, but this didn't seem very practical, and so he went with his plan C, which was to study environmental science. "I'd always been an outdoor type," he told me, "and I'd seen the beaches of my childhood turned into hotels. Where I'd taken paths through the bush, there was no bush anymore. At the rate things are going, I figured, this country is going to need environmentalists."

"And were your parents okay with that?" I asked.

"Of course not. They wanted me to become a doctor or something."

The particular problem for bird conservation in Jamaica is a lack of education. Although some NGOs are doing good work in this regard, there's not enough funding to introduce many schoolchildren to the country's natural heritage, and the university herpetologist and birdwatcher who once steered graduate students like Ricardo into ornithology has died. As a result, nobody except foreigners is studying birds now, and Ricardo, at thirty, is the youngest active member of the bird club.

The larger problems for Jamaican conservation are demographic, cultural, and economic. "I think our population is just getting out of *hand*," Ricardo said. "And that means more pressure on the environment. I always thought of our population as being two million, but suddenly I'm hearing that it's three million. It seemed to happen overnight."

"I heard it's three and a half million," I said.

"You see! Overnight!"

According to Ricardo, Jamaicans tend to be squeamish about wildlife. "They don't like anything creepy-crawly," he said. "Any snake will be chopped on sight. If they see a house lizard, they spray it with insect spray. They think the crocodiles are after them." Ricardo also believes that the recent influx of Chinese businessmen has aggravated this Jamaican mind-set. "Where Jamaicans formerly just killed crocodiles," he said, "now they're eating them. I know a research biologist who was studying a plat of tidal pool, and one day she got there and found a Chinese man with a knife, picking everything off the rocks and eating it. She was crying—she had to start a new plat."

I mentioned that South American countries with strong indigenous populations do a better job of protecting nature than those, like Chile, that are mostly populated by immigrants, and Ricardo agreed that Jamaica is more like Chile. "Jamaicans were brought here as slaves," he said. "The connection with nature seems to have been lost in the Middle Passage. They're all just looking for an easy buck. You get less than a hundred U.S. dollars if you poach a parrot. The parrot has much greater value if you leave it in the forest and bring guests to see it. But poachers will sometimes take the entire tree down to get the parrot nest, which is terrible for the parrots' population, because they're really dependent on old forest with natural nest holes. It's the same thing with sea turtles: Why kill a female that is coming in to lay hundreds of eggs? The same thing with lobsters: Why kill a gravid female?"

As part of his day job, Ricardo works with the island's hunters, who in late summer are permitted to shoot limited numbers of four dove and pigeon species. Hunters are natural allies of conservationists, but here, too, the country is haunted by its past. "Jamaicans look down on hunting," Ricardo said, "because colonialism left us with a hunting culture that's for rich people who have expensive weapons, with the poor people resenting them. There's a feeling that hunting is encouraged by the government while ordinary people can't have birds in cages—it's another way of sticking it to the poor people."

The best way past the economic obstacles to conservation is ecotourism. The Jamaica Tourist Board is now actively promoting Jamaica as a birdwatching destination and taking tour operators on informational trips, but a lot of money is needed to create a serious ecotouristic infrastructure, and without an infrastructure ecotourism can't generate a lot of money. And so the government itself continues to push for the development of all-inclusive mega-hotels, because these hotels generate jobs not by the handful but by the several hundred. "These mega-hotels are empty much of the time," Ricardo said, "and when a new hotel goes up it means an old one is going under. I personally think that permits for new hotels should be issued only if one hundred percent of existing hotels are one hundred percent full one hundred percent of the time."

I asked Ricardo if he kept his own bird list.

"I list," he said, with a guilty smile. "I confess that I list. I have something like one hundred eighty-eight species."

"Approximately one hundred eighty-eight."

He laughed and told me about an exhausted migrant warbler he'd found in September, on an early-morning beach walk. It was too tired to flee, so he'd photographed it with his cell phone. Later, at home, with the help of friends, he identified it as a Mourning Warbler. "So maybe," he said, "it's one eighty-nine now."

I was ready to go at five thirty the next morning, and when Ricardo failed to meet me in the hotel lobby I wondered if he was flakier than he'd seemed. But then he came running out of the darkness on the driveway and reported that he'd heard a Jamaican Owl and seen it fly into a tree. I hurried to get my flashlight. We couldn't find the telltale reflection of the owl's eyes in the foliage, but when the bird launched itself from the back of the tree I saw it well enough, with flashlight and binoculars, to identify it by its size and cinnamon plumage and general owliness before it disappeared.

Our destination was Ecclesdown Road, a narrow strip of pavement that winds up through the forested foothills of the John Crow Mountains. ("John Crow," the local name for the Turkey Vulture—a stoop-shouldered, red-faced, black-feathered bird— is said to derive from a stoop-shouldered preacher named John who once scoured the countryside for converts, wearing a long black coat, his face sunburned red.) Between intense rain showers, Ricardo and I walked for several miles and saw Jamaica's two endemic parrot species, three huge Chestnut-bellied Cuckoos, a group of Jamaican Crows (known locally as the Jabbering Crow, for its distinctive babbling voice), and, at the top of a tree, flashing its magenta underparts, a hummingbird called the Jamaican Mango.

Our top priority was the Crested Quail-Dove, a furtive ground dweller that Jamaicans call the Mountain Witch. It is threatened by habitat destruction and predation by the mongoose, an introduced mammal species, and is nearly as rare as the blackbird. When Ricardo finally heard one call, I got a useless, silhouetted glimpse of it flying low across the road. No sooner had we run to the spot where we'd seen it than the idyllic quiet of Ecclesdown Road was disrupted by a car, one of the first we'd seen all morning, honking its horn repeatedly. Two men appeared from the other direction, one carrying a heavy-duty chainsaw and the other a jug of gasoline. Almost immediately, the chainsaw started up in the woods downslope from us, followed soon by the crash of a large tree. We might not have spotted the quail-dove anyway, but the moment felt like a parable of conservation in a country with a dense population and little money. Although the land around us belonged to the government, much of it was under long-term private lease, and the forestry department lacks the resources to police illegal logging effectively. And so the Mountain Witch continues its retreat.

By the time Ricardo headed back to Kingston, I was missing only two endemics, the quail-dove and the lizard-cuckoo. I got up early again the next morning and walked Ecclesdown Road again, but rain was falling, harder and harder, and I saw nothing new before I had to leave for the airport. It was tempting to count my hearing of the cuckoo and my bad glimpse of the quail-dove and declare a sweep, but I followed the rules of the game and settled for having seen all but two of Jamaica's endemics. The standard consolation for failing to sweep is to tell yourself, "Oh, well, now I have a reason to come back to Jamaica," but realistically I knew that the next time I birded the Caribbean I'd want to go to islands with more unseen endemics to offer. Part of the appeal of the birding game is that failure is inevitable, since nobody will ever see every species on the planet; and games in which success can be assured are not worth playing. I'll probably never see the cuckoo or the quail-dove.

In Saint Lucia I was met at the airport by a retired firefighter, Olson Peter, who pointed out several firehouses on our drive from Castries to a bed-and-breakfast called A Peace of Paradise, on the Atlantic side of the island. Mindful of the mistake I'd made in Jamaica, I gave Peter a twenty-dollar tip and was surprised by the strange expression with which he pocketed it. Inside the bed-and-breakfast, my host, Lorraine Royall, explained that my fifty-dollar fare had not been prepaid, as I'd assumed from my Jamaican experience that it would be. She promised to get Peter his fifty dollars later, but my mistake was another ominous sign.

My guide the next morning was a young man named Melvin who materialized out of the pre-dawn twilight, like a genie, in a puff of cannabis smoke, while I was eating breakfast on Lorraine's back porch. Melvin was wearing rubber boots, rolled-up jeans, a thigh-length fishnet top, and a watch cap. Up the road from Lorraine's, he took me through a banana farm to a single Asian ornamental tree, a *pomme d'amour*, that was exploding in hot-pink flower and dripping with hummingbirds. Standing beneath its branches, on a thick carpet of hot pink, I didn't even need binoculars to identify the birds. Melvin and I then went down to the main coastal road and parked by an opening in the "dry" forest, which was dry only in comparison with the higher-altitude rain forest. Melvin put his thumb to his lips and did some rhythmic squeaking that instantly summoned up a pair of White-breasted Thrashers. They hopped around inquisitively in a tree above us, ascertained that we weren't thrashers, and disappeared again. True to their name, thrashers have an energetic presence and a lot of personality, and I was sorry to see them go.

The definition of a species—the category that bird listers depend on for their tabulations—is the subject of ongoing scientific debate. To divide the world of birdlife into discrete, Latin-named species is to impose a somewhat arbitrary grid on a fluid and supremely complex system of genes, crossbreeding, and evolution. Many of the Caribbean's endemics are nearly identical to more common mainland species but have evolved just enough, in their island isolation, to develop slightly different voices, plumages, structures, or habits. (The Jamaican Crow, for example, looked to me indistinguishable from the crows outside my window in Manhattan.) The Ornithologists' Union is forever revising its official taxonomy, "lumping" multiple species into a single species or "splitting" a single species into one or more new ones. Splitting can create what birders call an armchair lifer: you get a new life bird for your list without leaving your house. It's as if the definitions of a field goal and a touchdown were subject to indefinite revision, altering the outcomes of football games already played.

The White-breasted Thrasher, however, is not a gray-area species. With its dark back and its bright white front, it was like no other thrasher I'd seen. The bird was once common in both Martinique and Saint Lucia, but its range has shrunk dramatically as its habitat has been disturbed. There are now perhaps two hundred of them in Martinique, and the thousand or so individuals in Saint Lucia are concentrated in a small area of dry forest on the Atlantic coast. Seven years ago, the owners of a 554-acre property in the heart of the thrasher's range began to clear the land for a resort with the unfortunate (from a thrasher perspective) name of Le Paradis. The developers have since run into financial trouble, but not before driving most of the endangered thrashers off the property, carving out a golf course, and starting to erect several large building complexes. The unfinished buildings can be seen from the main road, falling apart, collecting rainwater, and looking like something military from a former war.

Later, when I flew back to New York, the plane would take me directly over Le Paradis and afford a view of the golf course, which is reverting to dense scrub—good habitat for many birds but not the forest-dwelling thrashers. I confess to feeling less than sorry for the developers. The JetBlue captain, speaking to us passengers, kept referring, annoyingly, to the "paradise" that we were leaving, and the first thing he said when we arrived in New York was "Welcome back to reality." It seemed to me that the captain had it exactly backward. Even in a deep recession, Americans enjoy fantastic luxuries that most West Indians do not, and despite strong political opposition we still do a good job of ensuring that the situation of our own endangered species is, if not paradisial, at least reasonably secure. Reality, in the form of unsustainable rates of population growth and tourist mega-development, is what lies to the south.

Melvin worked as a bird guide to supplement his income as a finder and researcher of plants for Saint Lucia's forestry department. He was likable and skilled at detecting birds in dense forest and luring them into view—we saw the lovely Saint Lucia Warbler and many other Lesser Antillean specialties, including the aptly named Gray Trembler—but he was hazy on the actual names of some of the species, and I thought it would be good, on my second full day in Saint Lucia, to pursue the remaining three endemics with a serious local birder whom Lorraine had arranged to guide me. The problem, Lorraine said, was that this birdwatcher was a Seventh Day Adventist and had not responded to her requests for confirmation and, indeed, since this was a Saturday, might not respond until nightfall.

Late in the afternoon, when the weather began to cool, I tried to drive to the Descartiers Nature Trail and see another endemic or two. Several roads ended abruptly in chasms created by landslides during Hurricane Tomas, and I got badly lost while searching for alternate routes, but I managed to reach the trailhead with forty-five minutes of daylight remaining. I ran down a trail with my binoculars and paused to look and listen at several clearings; but the rain forest, though well preserved, seemed empty of birds. Belatedly, I recalled one of the Fundamental Laws of Birding: *The best birds are always by the parking lot.* As I hurried back to my vehicle, I began to hear the cries of parrots returning to their roost, and, sure enough, in the parking lot, in failing light, I got a good look at a Saint Lucia Parrot flying over.

For dinner I went to the only nearby restaurant with a full bar. Sitting with drinks at another table on the veranda were a voluble Brit named Nigel, two young British women, and, to my surprise, the Adventist birdwatcher. Nigel produces nature films for the Discovery Channel, and it transpired that the Adventist was taking him birding the next day. Nigel invited me to join them, but he and I didn't have the same target species, and I was feeling sore with the Adventist for not having returned Lorraine's messages and for not being at home observing his religion. I sat down at a different table and listened to Nigel gratingly regale the girls with stories of the fabulous Lesser Antillean birds he'd seen. The Adventist came over and apologized to me, explaining that he'd thought I was coming a week later. I told him not to worry about it.

When I got back to A Peace of Paradise, Lorraine reported that the Adventist had just called her. "The first thing he said," she said, "was 'It's not my fault.' You get the dates in a text message and you write them down—how is that not his fault?"

I voiced my suspicion that the Adventist had found it more advantageous to go out with a Discovery Channel filmmaker.

"Hm, I hadn't thought of that," Lorraine said.

I assured her that I was very happy with Melvin.

The next morning, back at the Descartiers trailhead, we ran into Nigel and the Adventist and agreed to walk with them. The Adventist seemed like a nice enough man, and he certainly knew his birds; and Nigel, by burdening himself with a telescope and tripod on the trail, was showing himself to be not a dilettante or opportunistic birder but the real, avid, smitten thing. I mentioned to Melvin the poor impression that Nigel had made on me the night before, when he was drinking and impressing girls. Melvin nodded sympathetically: "He was excited." Using Nigel's scope, we had some fabulous looks at perching Saint Lucia Parrots, which have all the best parrot attributes: intense sociability, a rainbow of colors, gorgeous patterning on their heads and shoulders, and faces expressive of intelligence. Nigel's pleasure in studying them completed his redemption in my opinion.

It was starting to rain rather hard, though, and the Adventist was no more able than Melvin to conjure up birds that didn't feel like showing themselves. Still missing the endemic Saint Lucia Oriole and Saint Lucia Black Finch, I took Melvin back down to the drier coast. There, at the thrasher spot, by squeaking repeatedly, Melvin managed to entice one female black finch into view. Hearing Nigel and the Adventist crackling around in the brush above us, we scrambled up a muddy slope and saw Nigel up to his armpits in foliage, in country that I'd repeatedly been warned was infested with venomous fer-de-lances. He looked over his shoulder and gave me an insane smile, the smile of a kindred spirit, and the Adventist reported that they'd so far had only one bad glimpse of the White-breasted Thrasher. I decided not to mention that Melvin and I, the day before, had seen two of them extremely well here in less than half a minute.

I tried for the oriole again that afternoon, on the Descartiers trail, but the weather was foggy and rainy. By nightfall, I was very tired of failing to find the oriole, tired also of getting up every morning at 5:00 a.m., but I dutifully made plans to set out in the dark and give myself one more chance. When morning came, though, I didn't feel like getting out of bed. The thing about games is that you don't want to look too closely at why you're playing them. A great yawning emptiness underlies them, a close relative of the nothingness that lies beneath the surface of our busy lives. I'd already missed two endemics in Jamaica: what did it matter if I missed a Saint Lucian endemic, too? What did it matter, really, if I saw any birds at all?

I was rewarded for sleeping late by a tremendous rain shower from eight to nine o'clock—I couldn't have seen the oriole anyway, and I was happy to have a chance to catch up on my email. But then, as I worked on my email, the sun came out. Suddenly mindful of the birds I could see in the several hours before I had to be at the airport, I packed my bag in a rush and drove back to the dry-forest places that Melvin had shown me. The birds had been subdued by the rain and were only now becoming active. And how happy I was to see them! I found a new bird for my life list—the Caribbean Elaenia, supposedly "common" on Saint Lucia but hitherto unseen by me—but I was no less happy to see the now-familiar flycatchers and bullfinches. I'd met them only two days ago, and they already felt like old friends.

Farther down the coast, near the lighthouse at Vieux Fort, I watched a pair of frigatebirds fighting or courting aerially, directly over my head. I saw blue sky, blue ocean, green woods. A tropicbird sailing in leisurely loops above the water. Hummingbirds darting everywhere. I needed to head to the airport very soon, but I continued to walk the road slowly, still hoping for the Saint Lucia Oriole, still missing it.

THE REGULARS

(on the photographs of Sarah Stolfa)

Georgia Russell by Sarah Stolfa

didn't like these pictures at first sight. They reminded me of several personal defeats that I prefer not to dwell on, particularly my failure to survive in Philadelphia. I spent the worst year of my life in Philadelphia, and that's not said in hindsight: I was aware all along that I was having the worst year of my life. Philadelphia makes short work of a certain kind of ego; it refuses to flatter our sense of importance. It differs in this regard from the other great working-people's cities of the Northeast Corridor, Boston and Baltimore, whose powerful sense of identity is proudly performed by each succeeding generation. More TV shows are shot in one year in Baltimore and more movies in Boston than are shot in a decade in Philadelphia. Except for the mournful opening montage of empty streets, accompanied by a Springsteen dirge, there was nothing especially Philadelphian about Jonathan Demme's *Philadelphia*. Philly is all about absence, about losses, about the spaces in between. As an idea, it never achieved full reification. Even in the slummiest recesses of Brooklyn you can see the distant skyline of Manhattan and feel protected by it—protected from engulfment by your emotions, protected by the importance of New York. A glimpse of the Center City skyline from Kensington or Point Breeze, however, is just another reminder that there is nowhere better to go; it puts you in mind of underlit commuter-rail platforms, excess office space, the cavernous chill of City Hall, and our nation's cracked, silent Bell.

The city has done a little better in recent years. In the mid-nineties, though, to set foot outside your Philadelphian dwelling was to be assaulted by loneliness and by the kind of beauty that is loneliness's close cousin. An aesthetic experience unpolluted by robust identity. A beauty so pure it *hurt*. There was really almost nothing ugly anywhere in the Philly I knew. All of it—the winter-bitten grassy expanses of Logan Circle, the unreclaimed brownfields, the factories waiting their turn to be demolished, the plastic gas-station signage on Washington Street, the ghost of North Station, the seedy paraphernalia purveyors of South Street, the refineries and sewage-treatment facilities whose smell was the first thing to welcome visitors arriving from the city's conveniently but desolately situated airport—existed in splendid isolation, at the end of a century of depopulation and industrial decline, and insisted on being seen in its particularity. Even the parts of the city of which its tourist office was proudest, the Art Museum, Rittenhouse Square, were beset by the big sky and poor weather, by the summer haze and the notably biting winter winds, and lay close to the abysmal Delaware, and were themselves therefore lonely.

Plenty of people do live in Philadelphia, of course. And yet the population density is low by urban standards. When you see a person in New York, what you see is a New Yorker, one of many many. New Yorkers all share at least one story, which is that they are in New York. When you see a person in Philadelphia, you see an individual. You see a face unsurrounded by enough similar faces to be generalized about. You don't know the face's story but you know there's got to be a story there, and you have plenty of time to etch the face into your memory while you wait for a SEPTA bus to arrive or for the next face to loom up on the underpopulated streets of Mount Airy. Philadelphia is a city suited to the purest and most fundamental form of short story, the form as practiced by Chekhov and Trevor and Welty—writers whose reservoirs of empathy and curiosity are equal to the endless particularity of regular people's lives. Walking Philly's streets, I used to be consciously oppressed by the greatness and virtue of those writers, and to wish I had the heart to imagine my way into the regular human stories whose tantalizing exteriors I could see everywhere around me. I felt defeated by the insufficiency of my own courage or curiosity or brotherly love.

Looking at Sarah Stolfa's forty photographs of regular Philadelphians, I experienced this personal defeat afresh. There are no unsightly faces among Stolfa's Regulars. In fact, there are no faces that aren't extremely beautiful. Stolfa's images have the quality, shared by the city in which they were taken, of rendering the very concept of unsightliness nonsensical. Or, to put it more accurately, of reminding us of how instrumentally constituted our everyday notions of beauty really are. Philadelphia is ugly only to the extent that it fails to conform to what its beholder wants or approves of. This is why a beautiful Four Seasons resort erected on a formerly wildlife-friendly beach is ugly to me, the exurban sprawl of beautiful dream houses is ugly to me, and beautiful televised faces espousing abhorrent political views are ugly to me. And it is why, conversely, no animal or plant in nature is capable of ugliness unless we disapprove of it. The magic of good portraiture, such as Stolfa's, is to frame and de-reference human subjects in such a way as to evade our everyday aesthetic judgments and restore the subjects to a natural world in which everything is interesting, everything incites sympathy and wonder, everything is worth a careful second look. She's a classical short-storyist of the camera.

She is also very rock-and-roll. Rock at its best derives authenticity from immersion in the regular. The fact that no art form is more anxious and insecure about authenticity than rock may at first seem paradoxical, considering that no art form is more readily available to regular people. (All you need to make rock is a voice and/or the ability to play simple chords, the latter requiring little more than two functional hands, a double-digit IQ, and a few months' practice.) The problem is that as soon as a band becomes any good, its success and its expertise begin to feel like betrayals of the very thing that makes rock so great in the first place, its democratic availability to all. Much of mainstream music culture is dedicated to creating elaborate commercial lies to obfuscate the problem. (My favorite lyric along these lines sounds like it was written by Jennifer Lopez's publicist and is almost poignant in the nakedness of its image-management intentions: "Don't be fooled by the rocks that I got / I'm still, I'm still Jenny from the block.") A more appealing approach to the problem is the indie approach, which consists, essentially, of a band's resolutely continuing to be regular people making regular music. The Delta 72, the band that Stolfa played in while she worked her day job at the bar where these pictures were taken, released its first single with Dischord Records and Kill Rock Stars, the latter a label that enjoys ringing droll polemical changes on its name (Stars Kill Rock, Rock Stars Kill). In a thoroughly indie move, the Delta 72 relocated from Washington, D.C., a city that enjoyed at least a little notoriety as a birthplace of hardcore punk, to the deeply in-between and overlookable and therefore unimpeachably authentic city of Philadelphia. The indie aesthetic, or anti-aesthetic, is all over *The Regulars*: unnatural lighting, working-class stimulants, affordable clothes, tedious jobs, low-maintenance personal grooming, cash in small denominations, proximity to depression and alcoholism and other forms of quiet desperation, affinity for dive bars and other smoky, beat-up places; and yet, withal, not a *denial* of rock's glamour but rather a drastically democratic expansion of the field in which glamour might occur. Each subject in *The Regulars* gets to be the compelling star of his or her own frame, beautifully lit, with an almost studio-like blackness in the background and little nests of idiosyncracy in the foreground on the bartop.

Stolfa's inclusion of this bartop and its props, which lend the images both continuity and individuality, is cunning or felicitous. Here are a few statistics about what appears in her book's forty photographs:

Men: 27
Women: 13

Beer: 34
With whiskey: 4
With whiskey and a glass of water: 1
Wine: 2
Highball: 2
No drink: 2

Hat: 7
Headband: 1
Leafy hair ornament: 1
Clothing with text (including badges and buttons): 8
Tattoos: 4

Fairly unambiguous wedding band: 4
Clear or probable absence of wedding band: 19

Cash: 18
Purse: 5
Printed matter: 8
Stereo earphones: 1
Cell phone: 2
Cigarettes and/or lighter and/or active-looking
    ashtray: 25
Food: 1

To me the number that stands out here is the cigarette number, and it brings me to a third personal defeat: my inability to be the (indie? authentic?) sort of person who is comfortable in bars. The smoke problem has always been a big part of this, despite my own earlier twenty years of smoking, but even in smoke-free establishments I become miserable with self-consciousness and thrift and shame and shyness and etiquette anxiety, unless I'm part of a group. The result is that I can't look at *The Regulars* without envy and longing—a wish to be one of the Regulars myself. The book is personal in that way. Implicit in its title is the relation to the photographer in which each subject stands. The twenty-five of them who are looking straight into the lens aren't just looking at some shutterbug, they're looking at their regular bartender, Sarah Stolfa. They may be lonely, but I'm the one who feels it.

INVISIBLE LOSSES

magine a slender mouse-gray bird, no bigger than a starling, that spends most of its life on open ocean. In cold water and all weather, the Ashy Storm Petrel—a warm-blooded animal that weighs less than an ounce and a half—forages among the waves for tiny fish and ocean invertebrates. Fluttering with dangled legs, its toes skimming the surface, it gives the impression of walking on water, like the biblical Peter.

Although an even smaller cousin species, Wilson's Storm Petrel, is one of the world's most abundant and widespread birds, Ashies are rare and restricted to California waters. They have a distinctive strong musky odor; you can smell them in the fog. They're most at home on the water, but, like all birds, they need to be on land to lay eggs and raise their young. For this, they prefer undisturbed islands. To escape the attention of predators, they nest underground, in rock crevices or burrows, and come and go only at night.

In the Farallon Islands National Wildlife Refuge, thirty miles west of San Francisco's Golden Gate, a local artists' collective has built a kind of sloppy igloo out of chunks of concrete from the ruins of old buildings on the main island. A small door in the sculpture allows access to a crawl space lined with plexiglass. If you go in there on a summer night and shine a red light (less disturbing to birds than white light), you might see an Ashy Storm Petrel sitting patiently on an egg at the bottom of its crevice, looking even smaller and frailer than it would on the water. You might hear the nocturnal song of one of its hidden neighbors, a soft and tuneful purr that emerges from the rocks like a voice from another world: the world of seabirds, which encompasses two-thirds of our planet but is mostly invisible to us. Until recently, invisibility was an advantage for seabirds, a cloak of protection. But now, as they disappear from the oceans, they need people to protect them; and it's difficult to care about animals you can't see.

The Farallons today are a small portal to the past, when seabirds were abundant everywhere. More than half a million birds were nesting in the reserve when I visited the main island in June. On steep slopes and sparsely vegetated level ground, surrounded by deep-blue water roiling with seals and sea lions, were puffins and guillemots and cormorants, tiny plump Cassin's Auklets, weirdly horned Rhinoceros Auklets, and, in my opinion, way too many Western Gulls. The gull chicks were hatching, and it was impossible to walk anywhere without enraging their parents, which screamed at ear-hurting volumes and jumped into the air to strafe intruders with evil-smelling excrement.

The gulls were a gauntlet worth running to reach the island's colonies of Common Murre. One morning, Pete Warzybok, a biologist with Point Blue, the conservation group that helps the U.S. Fish and Wildlife Service monitor wildlife in the Farallons, led me up to a plywood blind overlooking a murre metropolis. Like a blanket of coarsely ground pepper, twenty thousand black-and-white birds covered a sloping spit of rock that bottomed out in surf-splashed cliffs. The murres were standing shoulder to shoulder, pointy-billed, penguin-like, and incubating an egg or guarding a tiny chick on territories as small as a few square inches. The colony had an air of quiet industry. There were occasional outbursts of gentle clucking, and the menacing gulls kept sailing over, scanning for breakfast opportunities, and sometimes a murre landing awkwardly or scrambling to take flight would scuffle with a neighbor. But the disputes ended as suddenly as they started, the birds resuming their grooming as if nothing had happened.

"Murres do what murres do," Warzybok remarked. "They aren't the brightest birds."

What murres do is exercise devotion. Although divorce is not unheard-of, they form strong pair-bonds and may live for thirty-five years, returning every year to the same tiny territory and raising one chick. Parents share incubation duties equally, one of them remaining in the colony while the other ranges over the ocean and dives underwater for anchovies, juvenile rockfish, or whatever else is available. When a bird returns from a long foraging trip, the parent that has stayed behind—increasingly hungry and streaked with guano—is still reluctant to leave the egg. In the literature of murres, there's an anecdote of a mother whose egg rolled downhill as soon as she laid it. A gull came by and swallowed it, stood for a moment with an enormous lump in its throat, and then regurgitated the egg, which rolled farther downslope and hit a standing murre, which promptly climbed onto it and began to incubate it. "If they don't have an egg," Warzybok said, "they'll incubate a stone or a piece of vegetation. They'll lay a fish on an unhatched egg, trying to feed it. And they won't give up. They'll sit on a dead egg for seventy-five or eighty days, the two birds trading incubation shifts."

Murre chicks take to the water when they're barely three

weeks old, too young to fly or dive. Their fathers go with them and stay by their side for months, feeding them and teaching them to fish while their mothers, which have made a heavy caloric investment in producing eggs, go off by themselves to recover. Parental devotion and the equal division of labor pay dividends. The reproductive success rate of Farallon murres is extremely high, typically above seventy percent, and they're one of the most abundant breeding seabirds in North America. Huge though it was, the colony that Warzybok and I were visiting held less than five percent of the islands' murres.

The murre population today represents a provisionally happy ending to a long, sad story. Two hundred years ago, when Russian hunters began wiping out Californian fur seals, as many as three million murres bred in the Farallons. In 1849, when the Gold Rush made San Francisco a boomtown, the islands became an inviting target for a city without a poultry industry. By 1851, the Farallone Egg Company was gathering half a million murre eggs a year for sale to bakeries and restaurants. Its eggers arrived by boat in the spring, crushed the eggs that had already been laid, and proceeded to collect every freshly laid one. Over the next half century, at least fourteen million murre eggs were harvested on the Farallons. The birds' fidelity to their nest sites kept them coming back, year after year, to be robbed of the objects of their devotion.

By 1910, fewer than twenty thousand murres remained on the main island. Even after egging stopped, they fell victim to the cats and dogs introduced by the keepers of the island's lighthouse, and large numbers were killed at sea by oil flushed from the tanks of ships entering San Francisco Bay. The murre population didn't seriously recover until after 1969, when the main island became a federal wildlife refuge. And then, in the early 1980s, the population plunged again.

The problem was the indiscriminate fishing method known as gill-netting. Hauling a huge net to the surface of the ocean sweeps up not only the target fish but porpoises, otters, turtles, and diving seabirds. Today, globally, at least 400,000 seabirds are killed every year in gill nets—murres and puffins and diving-ducks in northern waters, penguins and diving-petrels off the coast of South America. The annual worldwide toll on murres alone may exceed the 146,000 killed in the 1989 *Exxon Valdez* oil spill, the most destructive spill in history.

Beginning in the mid-1980s, many American states, including California, took note of the ecological havoc and imposed severe restrictions or outright bans on gill-netting. The result, in the Farallons, was an immediate surge in seabird numbers. In the past fifteen years, safe from gill-netting, and free to do what they do, the murres have quadrupled their population. The only threat to their survival in the Farallons now is the disruption of their food source by climate change or overfishing.

Pete Warzybok, perched in the blind, was writing down the species of fish that the murres in his study plot brought back to their nests. To a California fisherman asked to share the ocean's bounty with seabirds—Farallon murres consume more than 50,000 metric tons of fish every summer—the argument for murre conservation isn't just ethical or aesthetic. The birds that Warzybok studies function like airborne fishery-monitoring devices, a fleet of living research drones. They scour thousands of square miles of ocean and are expert at finding where the food is. Using only binoculars and a notebook, Warzybok can gather better data about current anchovy and rockfish populations, for much less money, than California's fishery managers can gather from a boat.

Farallon murres are the lucky ones. They've survived most of the major threats to seabirds, and a case can be made for their economic utility. Elsewhere, globally, in the past sixty years, the overall seabird population is estimated to have fallen by seventy percent. This number is even worse than it sounds, because a disproportionate number of seabird species are at risk of extinction. Of the world's 350 or so seabirds, a larger percentage is listed as endangered or threatened than of any comparable group of birds. Parrots, as a group, have troubles of their own, but they're also widely admired. Game birds are valuable to hunters; eagles and other raptors are conspicuous and iconic. Seabirds breed on remote, forbidding islands and spend most of their lives in waters inhospitable to us. If they disappeared entirely, how many people would even notice?

Imagine a young albatross in the South Atlantic Ocean. It's following the circumpolar winds, gliding five hundred miles a day on its ten-foot wingspan, using its nose to track the smell of fish or squid or crustraceans near the water's surface. Often the best place to find food is in the wake of a deepwater fishing vessel. The young albatross glides in circles around a trawler and eyes the chaos of smaller seabirds tussling over the fish scraps thrown overboard. When it plunges into the scrum, it brings a size advantage: a massive bill and a wingspan that announces, *I am huge!* The other birds scatter, but as the albatross hits the water something goes terribly wrong. Its outstretched wings have wrapped around the cable of the trawler's net, which drags it under and swiftly pulls it deeper. No one sees this happen. No one is out on the cold, choppy water except the trawler's crew. Even if the crew had time to be looking, the bird has disappeared in the blink of an eye, and its dead body won't float to the surface until the ship has moved on.

Every year, thousands of albatrosses are killed invisibly by trawlers. Tens of thousands more die on the hooks of long-line fishing vessels, along with even greater numbers of petrels and shearwaters. Accidental death in the world's fisheries is one of the two most grievous threats that seabirds face, and it's a tough one to address, because deepwater fishing boats typically operate under intense financial pressure and minimal oversight. Only a few countries seriously regulate their fleets' seabird bycatch.

In one of those countries, South Africa, I met a successful long-line tuna-boat captain named Deon van Antwerpen. With me, at a small harbor in Cape Town, was Ross Wanless, a biologist who manages the seabird conservation program of BirdLife South Africa. Wanless had come to the harbor to hear about the problems that Van Antwerpen was having with the government's seabird regulations. Van Antwerpen, a beefy and voluble man, gestured unhappily toward a basket of pale green fishing-line weights at the back of his vessel. "We've lost three thousand of these things," he said.

Long-line fishing kills albatrosses differently than trawling does. A smaller seabird dives down and brings a baited hook to the surface and tries to pull the bait off, and then an albatross barges in and swallows the whole thing, hooking itself and drowning. One solution is to weight the line, so that the baited hook quickly sinks out of reach of the birds. But a bare metal sinker can become a bullet to a crew member's forehead when a hundred-pound tuna is hauled in and the line recoils. BirdLife recommends sinkers with a loosely attached casing of luminescent plastic (light attracts fish), and Van Antwerpen had been eager to try them on his vessel. "Every bird I catch," he said to Wanless, "is potentially a fish I didn't catch. But you need to get legislation that's practical. If you don't, then most guys will just ignore it."

There ensued an intricate discussion between an exceptionally conscientious boat owner and a conservationist whose goal is to bring bird-safe methods to the entire world's deep-sea fishing fleet. Van Antwerpen's chief complaint with the plastic sinkers was that BirdLife wanted them too close to the baited hook—"If a shark snaps the line, we lose the sinker." Would it be okay if he increased the separation between sinker and hook to four meters? Wanless frowned and pointed out that this would make the hook sink too slowly to protect seabirds. But maybe increasing the weight of the sinker would compensate for a greater separation? Van Antwerpen said he'd be happy to do the experiment—he really didn't want to catch albatrosses. He just wanted to catch tuna without losing all his sinkers.

Fishing vessels can further reduce seabird bycatch by dragging a "bird-scaring" line, which consists of a brightly tasseled rope with a plastic cone at the end of it. Bird-scaring lines are inexpensive, easy to use, and highly effective at keeping birds out of a vessel's wake. A trawler, by using only a bird-scaring line, can reduce albatross mortality by as much as ninety-nine percent. Because a long-line vessel's hooks remain close to the surface beyond the bird-scaring line, South Africa requires it to take one additional protective measure, either weighting its lines or setting them after dark, when the birds are less active and can't see the bait.

Wanless and his wife, Andrea Angel, who is the leader of BirdLife's Albatross Task Force, have been working with South Africa's government and fishing fleet for more than a decade.

Any commercial vessel fishing in South African waters now has to practice seabird-bycatch mitigation, and Wanless and Angel are attempting to forge relationships with every skipper in the country's fleet. "The way to achieve something," Wanless told me, "is not to present a fancy technical solution but to engage with human beings." As a result of his and Angel's efforts, the annual toll on seabirds in South Africa has fallen from an estimated 35,000 in 2006 to as few as 3,000 today. The trawler fleet in neighboring Namibia has reduced its bycatch from 20,000 to 1,000.

But protecting seabirds takes more than regulations. It also requires independent monitoring of fishing vessels and, ideally, a financial incentive for the industry to reduce seabird bycatch. Although long-liners have one straightforward reason to catch fewer birds—"They'd rather catch ten-thousand-dollar bills, which is what a bluefin tuna represents," Wanless said—a potentially stronger incentive is the market for sustainably harvested fish. Pursuit of this premium market, particularly in Europe, has led much of South Africa's fleet to pay to put an observer on each of its ships, to ensure compliance with bycatch rules. Without an observer on board, even a captain like Van Antwerpen may sometimes break the rules.

The best way for a government to ensure compliance is to mandate that every vessel be outfitted with a digital camera to monitor its catch and bycatch. When Australia did this with its tropical tuna-fishing fleet, in 2016, ship captains placed panicked calls to Australian regulators, asking where they could buy bird-scaring lines. "Once there's a camera on board, the game's over," Wanless said. "You're risking losing your license for failing to buy a hundred dollars' worth of gear."

Another promising technological advance is the Hookpod, which Wanless calls "the silver bullet." It consists of a hard plastic case that snaps around a baited hook, protecting the bait from birds and birds from the hook, and that doesn't spring open until it has sunk to a safe depth. The Hookpod isn't as cheap as a hook and a sinker, but it's cheap compared with the value of tuna, and it comes with an LED that attracts them. "What we like about the Hookpod," Van Antwerpen told me, "is that we put six of them in the water and caught fish with two of them, because of the light."

It is theoretically possible, by making the Hookpod standard equipment on all long-line vessels, and by requiring all trawlers to run bird-scaring lines, and by simply banning gill-net fishing (as South Africa has done), to render the world's oceans safe for seabirds. For now, though, the global situation remains atrocious. Wanless and Angel have expanded their outreach to the fisheries of South America, Korea, and Indonesia, with not altogether discouraging results, but the fleets of China and Taiwan, which together account for two-thirds of fishing vessels on the high seas, operate with little or no regard for seabird mortality, and they sell their catch in markets mostly indifferent to sustainability. Wanless estimates that 300,000 seabirds, including 100,000 albatrosses, continue to be killed annually by long-liners alone. This is hard enough on the abundant species, like Sooty Shearwaters. But many species of albatross, which are slow to reach maturity and typically breed only in alternate years, are threatened with extinction. And, as harmful as modern fishing practices are, there's an even deadlier threat that seabirds face.

Gough Island, a twenty-five-square-mile mass of volcanic rock in the South Atlantic Ocean, is home to millions of breeding seabirds, including the entire world population of the Atlantic Petrel and all but a few pairs of the critically endangered Tristan Albatross. Ross Wanless first went to Gough in 2003, as a doctoral candidate, after other researchers had reported that alarmingly few petrels and albatrosses were fledging chicks. It was known that rats and cats, which humans have introduced on islands all over the world, prey heavily on seabirds. But there were no rats or cats on Gough, only mice. Using video cameras and infrared lights, Wanless recorded what the mice were doing to the petrel chicks. "The sun went down," he said, "and a mouse came out in the petrel burrow. It hesitated and then started nibbling on the chick. Other mice came, and I witnessed this insane, disgusting attack. As the blood started to flow, the mice got more and more excited. At times, there were four or five of them competing for the wound, lapping up blood and going inside to eat the chick's internal organs."

Having evolved without terrestrial predators, seabirds have no defense against mice. A petrel in its inky-dark burrow can't even see what's happening to its chick, and an albatross on its nest lacks the instinct to recognize mice as a threat. In 2004, Wanless recorded 1,353 breeding failures among Gough's Tristan Albatrosses, most of them from mice predation, and only about 500 successes; in more recent years, the rate of breeding failure has been as high as ninety percent. Among all species of seabird on Gough, mice now kill two million chicks every year, and many of these species are also losing adults in the fisheries. Annual mortality among adult Tristan Albatrosses at sea has risen to ten percent—more than triple the rate of natural mortality. Ten percent adult mortality plus ninety percent breeding failure is a formula for extinction.

The calamitous decline in seabird populations has many

causes. Overfishing of anchovies and other small prey fish directly deprives penguins and gannets and puffins of the energy they need to reproduce. Overfishing of tuna, schools of which drive smaller fish to the ocean's surface, can make it more difficult for shearwaters and petrels to forage. Climate change, which alters ocean currents, already appears to be causing breeding failure among Iceland's puffins, and birds that nest on low-lying islands are vulnerable to rising sea levels. Plastic pollution, particularly in the Pacific Ocean, is clogging the guts of seabirds and leaving them hungry for real food. And the resurgence of marine mammal populations—in other respects, an environmental success story—has resulted in more seals to eat young penguins, more sea lions to crowd cormorants out of their breeding sites, and more whales to compete with diving birds for prey.

The number-one threat to seabirds, however, is introduced predators: rats, cats, and mice overrunning the islands where they breed. This is the bad news. The good news is that invasive species are a problem with achievable solutions. Organizations such as Island Conservation, a nonprofit based in California, have perfected the use of helicopters and GIS technology to target predators with mammal-specific poisoned bait. Animal lovers may grieve at the mass killing of small furry mammals, but human beings have an even greater responsibility to the species they've threatened with extinction, however inadvertently, by introducing predators.

The most ambitious rodent-eradication effort to date was mounted by the South Georgia Heritage Trust. South Georgia island, which lies nine hundred miles from the Antarctic Peninsula, is the breeding ground of perhaps thirty million seabirds;

without rats and mice, the island could easily host three times that number. From 2011 to 2015, at a cost of more than $10 million, three helicopters traversed every ice-free area on South Georgia, dropping bait. No living rat or mouse has been detected since 2015.

Similar efforts are now planned for Gough Island, in 2019, and for South Africa's Marion Island in 2020. Mice came to Marion with whaling and sealing vessels in the nineteenth century. In the 1940s, the South African government introduced cats to control them, and the cats quickly went feral. Instead of killing mice, they proceeded to decimate the smaller seabird species nesting on the island. ("Mice know exactly what a cat is," Ross Wanless explained. "Seabirds don't.") Marion's seabird populations were expected to recover as soon as the last cats were removed from it, in 1991, but they didn't. "The mice are the only explanation," Wanless said.

Seabirds are a poignant combination of extreme vulnerability and extreme toughness. A twenty-pound Tristan Albatross can't stop a one-ounce mouse from eating its young, and yet it thrives in frigid saltwater and brutal winds and can bully a large gull. Because of its longevity, it may survive twenty years of breeding failure and still produce chicks, once the threat to its nest is eliminated. "Seabirds respond well to restoration," Nick Holmes, the science director at Island Conservation, told me. "Addressing the terrestrial threat bolsters their resistance to all the other threats." When Island Conservation and its partners eliminated rats from California's Anacapa Island, south of Santa Barbara, the hatching success rate of Scripps's Murrelet (a small cousin of the Common Murre) immediately jumped from thirty percent to eighty-five percent. The murrelets are now secure on

Anacapa, and Ashy Storm Petrels have been recorded breeding there for the first time.

To prevent the extinction of a species, you first have to know that it exists. You need ocular proof, and seabirds are especially adept at withholding it. Consider the story of the Magenta Petrel. In 1867, an Italian research vessel, the *Magenta*, shot a single specimen of a large gray-and-white petrel in the South Pacific. For more than a century, this remained the only scientific evidence of the species. But invisibility is enticing, and in 1969 an amateur ornithologist named David Crockett went to New Zealand's Chatham Islands to search for the bird. Although much of the Chathams' main island had been cleared for pasture by European and Maori farmers, its southwest corner was still forested, and there were piles of unidentified petrel bones in the middens of a Polynesian people, the Moriori, who had settled the islands centuries earlier. Crockett had read accounts of latter-day Moriori collecting and eating a large petrel, known locally as taiko, as late as 1908. He suspected that the taiko was the Magenta Petrel, and that it might still be nesting in burrows in the forest.

The tract of forest where the Moriori had collected taiko was owned by a sheep farmer of Maori descent, Manuel Tuanui. Inspired by the prospect of discovering a lost native bird on their land, Tuanui and his teenage son, Bruce, helped Crockett conduct a series of arduous searches for the taiko, scouring the forest for burrows and setting up spotlights to attract seabirds flying in at night. To Bruce, Crockett was "this strange guy who was chasing a *taipo* [a Maori word for ghost]." When Bruce married a young woman from a neighboring island, Liz Gregory-Hunt, she was swept up in his family's quest for the taiko. "You get sucked into the vortex," she told me, "and it becomes your life."

On the night of January 3, 1973, Crockett was rewarded with a spotlighted look at four birds that matched the description of the Magenta Petrel: ocular proof. But he also wanted to capture taiko and find where they nested, and this was even harder than seeing them. It was another five years before Bruce and Liz, driving into town from the farm, were stopped on the road by an uncle of Bruce's who gave them the news: "They've just caught two taiko." It was a further ten years before Crockett and a team of scientists were able to locate two active taiko burrows in the forest, by radio-tracking captured birds.

For the Tuanuis, this was still only the beginning. The taiko's single known breeding site was on their land, and the bird needed to be protected from the threats that had already nearly driven it extinct. Lines of traps were set around the burrows for nonnative cats and opossums, and Manuel Tuanui, in a move considered "mental" by his neighbors, donated 2,900 acres of bush to the New Zealand government, which fenced most of the land against sheep and cattle. Within a few years, because of the family's efforts, the number of pairs of taiko known to breed in the forest began to rise; today it stands at more than twenty.

On a hot day in January, I joined a British seabird specialist, Dave Boyle, and a British volunteer worker, Giselle Eagle, on a long trek to the burrow of a female taiko known to them as S64. She was incubating an egg fertilized by a male taiko that had lived in the area for eighteen seasons before finally attracting a mate. Boyle wanted to examine S64 before her egg hatched and she began to spend more time foraging at sea. "There's no way of knowing how old she is," he said. "She could have been breeding somewhere else with a different partner, or she could be very young."

The terrain was rugged, the forest dense and intermittently boggy. S64's burrow was tucked into a steep hillside covered thickly with ferns and tree litter. Boyle kneeled down and removed the lid of an underground wooden nest box previously installed at the back end of the burrow. Peering in, he shook his head sadly. "It looks like the chick got stuck hatching."

Chick death is not uncommon, especially if the mother is young and inexperienced, but every breeding failure is a setback for a species whose total population is still only about two hundred. Boyle reached into the box and lifted out S64. She was big for a petrel but seemed small in his hands, and she had no idea of how rare and precious she was; she squirmed and tried to bite Boyle until he slipped her into a cloth bag. To discourage her from hanging around the burrow any longer, he removed the dead chick and the crumpled shell that had trapped its legs. Working with Eagle, he then fastened a band to S64's leg, stuck her with a needle to draw a DNA sample, and shot a microchip under the skin on her back.

"She's not having a good day," Eagle said.

"Once she's got a microchip in," Boyle said, "we never have to handle her again."

The few taikos that survived centuries of predation and habitat loss nested deep in the forest because it was relatively safe, not because it was an optimal site. To get airborne, even adult taiko need to climb a tree, and it can take a new fledgling several days to fight its way out of the forest, a struggle that may leave it too weak to survive on the ocean. When the Tuanui family created a formal organization, the Chatham Island Taiko

Trust, in 1998, one of its aims was to raise off-island money for a fully predator-proof enclosure much closer to the water. The enclosure, called Sweetwater, was completed in 2006, and many of the chicks now born in the forest are transferred to Sweetwater before fledging, to "imprint" the location on their memory and encourage them to return there to breed. The first Sweetwater-imprinted taiko returned in 2010; many more have returned since then.

The Taiko Trust has also transferred chicks of the Chatham Petrel, a bird smaller and scarcely less endangered than the taiko, from a nearby island to Sweetwater, to create a secure alternate nesting site for the species. To bolster the population of the Chatham Albatross, a species whose only colony is on Te Tara Koi Koia, a constricting offshore cone of rock also known as the Pyramid, the Trust has ferried three hundred chicks to a second predator-proof enclosure on the main island, above the majestic sea cliffs on the Tuanui farm. "For the Trust to survive," Liz Tuanui said, "we knew we had to diversify to other species."

Liz has now spent four decades in the vortex. She chairs the Taiko Trust, and she and Bruce have fenced thirteen tracts of forest altogether, seven of them entirely at their own expense. This has benefited both seabirds and the native flora and land birds—the splendid Chatham Pigeon, once close to extinction on the main island, now numbers more than a thousand—but Bruce prefers to emphasize the synergy between conservation and farming. Fencing the forest, he told me, also protects his waterways, provides shelter for his stock during storms, and makes it easier for him to muster his sheep. When I pressed him to account for why a sheep-farming family had shouldered the burden of saving three of the world's rarest seabirds, at such a cost of labor and money, he demurred with a shrug. "If we didn't do it," he said, "no one else was going to do it. Finding the taiko was a huge effort. It was part of us but part of the Chathams, too—it created a lot of interest all over the island."

"It's awesome," Liz said. "We have tenfold the number of people protecting their bush than twenty-five years ago."

"If we don't do it," Bruce said, "it's going to be even harder for the next generation."

The crucial difference between the Chatham Islands and the world in which most of us live, it seemed to me, is that islanders don't need to struggle to imagine seabirds. From the Taiko Trust's predator-proof cliffside enclosure, to which young Chatham Albatrosses will soon be returning to court their mates, it's only a two-hour boat trip out to Te Tara Koi Koia. There, on vertiginous slopes, above blue ocean swells heaving against kelp-covered rocks, stern-browed albatross parents attend to their downy gray chicks. Overhead, in such numbers that they confuse your sense of scale and seem no bigger than seagulls, the albatrosses circle and ride the wind on their immense wings. Very few people will ever see them.

9/13/01

The one recurring nightmare I've had for many years is about the end of the world, and it goes like this. In a crowded, modern cityscape not unlike lower Manhattan, I'm flying a jetliner down an avenue where everything is wrong. It seems impossible that the buildings to either side of me won't shear my wings off, impossible that I can keep the plane aloft while moving at such a low speed. The way is always blocked, but somehow I manage to turn a sharp corner or to pilot the plane beneath an overpass, only to confront a skyscraper so high that I would have to rise vertically to clear it. As I pull the plane into a dismayingly shallow climb, the skyscraper looms and rushes forward to meet me, and I wake up, with unspeakable relief, in my ordinary bed.

On Tuesday there was no awakening. You found your way to a TV and watched. Unless you were a very good person indeed, you were probably, like me, experiencing the collision of several incompatible worlds inside your head. Besides the horror and sadness of what you were watching, you might also have felt a childish disappointment over the disruption of your day, or a selfish worry about the impact on your finances, or admiration for an attack so brilliantly conceived and so flawlessly executed, or, worst of all, an awed appreciation of the visual spectacle it produced.

Never mind whether certain Palestinians were or were not

dancing in the streets. Somewhere—you can be absolutely sure of this—the death artists who planned the attack were rejoicing over the terrible beauty of the towers' collapse. After years of dreaming and working and hoping, they were now experiencing a fulfillment as overwhelming as any they could have allowed themselves to pray for. Perhaps some of these glad artists were hiding in ruined Afghanistan, where the average life expectancy is barely forty. In that world, you can't walk through a bazaar without seeing men and children who are missing limbs.

In this world, where the Manhattan skyline has now been maimed and the scorched wreckage at the Pentagon is reminiscent of Kabul, I'm trying to imagine what I don't want to imagine: the scene inside a plane one moment before impact. At the controls, a terrorist is raising a prayer of thanks to Allah in expectation of instant transport from this world to the next one, where houris will presently reward him for his glorious success. At the back of the cabin, huddled Americans are trembling and moaning and, no doubt, in many cases, praying to their God for a diametrically opposite outcome. And then, a moment later, for hijacker and hijacked alike, the world ends.

On the street, after the impact, survivors spoke of being delivered from death by God's guidance and grace. But even they, the survivors, were stumbling out of the smoke into a different world. Who would have guessed that everything could end so suddenly on a pretty Tuesday morning? In the space of two hours, we left behind a happy era of Game Boy economics and trophy houses and entered a world of fear and vengeance. Even if you'd been waiting for the nineties-ending crash throughout the nineties, even if you'd believed all along that further terrorism in New York was only a matter of when and not of whether, what you felt on Tuesday morning wasn't intellectual satisfaction, or simply empathetic horror, but deep grief for the loss of daily life in prosperous, forgetful times: the traffic jammed by delivery trucks and unavailable cabs, *Apocalypse Now Redux* in local theaters, your date for drinks downtown on Wednesday, the sixty-three homers of Barry Bonds, the hourly AOL updates on J. Lo's doings. On Monday morning, the front-page headline in the *Daily News* had been KIPS BAY TENANTS SAY: WE'VE GOT KILLER MOLD. This front page is (and will, for a while, remain) amazing.

The challenge in the old world, the nineties world of Bill Clinton, was to remember that, behind the prosperity and complacency, death was waiting and entire countries hated us. The problem of the new world, the zeroes world of George Bush, will be to reassert the ordinary, the trivial, and even the ridiculous in the face of instability and dread: to mourn the dead and then try to awaken to our small humanities and our pleasurable daily nothing-much.

POSTCARDS FROM EAST AFRICA

When I was home and talking to my brother Bob, he asked me whether an East African safari was something a person *had to do*. Certain well-traveled friends of his—competitive vacationers; proponents of the Bucket List—had assured him that it was. Did I agree?

I certainly share Bob's irritation with the Bucket List thing. We're put off by the blatancy of its consumerism, the glibness of its realism. If you were truly, depressively realistic, you'd recognize that checking boxes on a list won't make death any less final or undesirable; that none of the experiences we've racked up in life will matter when we've kicked the bucket and returned to eternal nothingness. Bucket Listers seem to imagine that death can be cheated by strategic vacationing.

"Some of the country is amazingly beautiful," I said. "The Ngorongoro Crater is like no other place on earth."

"But you wouldn't say it's something I *have to do*," Bob said.

"Not at all. You should do whatever you want."

I was telling him what he wanted to hear. In fact, though, I *had* found it imperative to go to East Africa. Having gone there to see birds did set me apart from the Bucket Listers. But this only changed the terms of the question of why I travel. It didn't answer it.

Consider the French sociologist Jean Baudrillard's theory of the simulacrum—the idea that consumer capitalism has replaced reality with representations of reality. Unless you travel by helicopter or single-engine plane, it's impossible to escape the contrast between East Africa's clean and lushly vegetated parks, teeming with wildebeests and elephants, and the overgrazed, overpopulated, trash-strewn countrysides that separate them: the hegemony of Coca-Cola, the heavily guarded Del Monte pineapple plantations, the rail lines and highways that Chinese engineers are building to speed the extraction of soda ash and coal, the specters of AIDS and Islamic terrorism. The parks function as simulacra in which tourists, most of them white, all of them affluent, can "experience" an "Africa" whose representation is contingent on their money. The baobabs and the acacias are native, and at night the southern constellations are unfamiliar to northerners; this much is genuine. But, in the same way that people in a real blizzard now exclaim that it looks just like a blizzard in a movie, you may find yourself viewing zebras in the Serengeti and recalling the zebras in a safari park in Florida. Not only is the real thing not real, it strikes you as a copy of a copy. The Serengeti suffers further from having been the setting of so many nature films. The image of a lion bringing down a gazelle is a cliché to anyone who grew up watching National Geographic documentaries. Worse yet, the fact that it's a cliché is also a cliché. What added value, exactly, does the tourist receive from distantly glimpsing dramatic scenes of life and death that he or she can see extremely well at home? Does the world really need more amateur photographs of giraffes?

And then, for me, the problem of mammals. To secure the company of my other brother, Tom, and of a good college friend, also named Tom, I'd promised them that we'd see a ton of furry wildlife on the trip, not just birds. But in my communications with the trip's organizers, Rockjumper Birding Tours, I'd emphasized that if I had to choose between looking at a cheetah and studying a dumpy little brown warbler, I'd choose the warbler.

I'm told that most people prefer mammals to birds because we ourselves are mammals. This seems to me both reasonable and questionable. If the great attraction of nature is its Otherness, why do we need our close kindred to make it interesting? Isn't this sort of embarrassingly self-infatuated? Birds, with their dinosaur lineage and their flight capabilities, are truly Other. And yet, being conspicuous bipeds like us, and responding, like us, primarily to sight and sound, they're arguably *more* similar to us than other mammals, which tend to be furtive and four-legged and to live in a world defined by smell.

For the mammal lover, a young elephant in a well-designed zoo is no less adorable than a young elephant in an African nature park; the only value added by the latter is that the elephant is plucking its own grass, that it behaves as if it's at risk of attack by lions, and that the boundaries of the park are too far away to see. Caging a bird in an aviary, however, negates its very essence; an eagle is nothing if you can't see it soar. To experience African birds, you have to go to Africa.

If, as we're told, the point of exotic travel is to "create memories," and if, as I would insist, our memories consist fundamentally of good stories, and if what makes a story good is some element of unexpectedness, it follows that the point of traveling is to be surprised. My brother Tom was surprised to arrive in Nairobi and learn that his checked baggage was still at Dulles International Airport. His four-day wait to be reunited with his suitcase will be front and center in both his memory and his stories of our trip.

One easy way to manufacture surprise is to not do your homework. I was surprised, for example, to discover that the tsetse fly is not an insidious, nocturnal, mosquito-like insect but a large and aggressive diurnal biting fly. My bad. But I'll remember those flies, as well as the leather-handled ox tail that our Tanzanian driver and local bird expert, Geitan, used to shoo them off his back and out of our Land Cruiser.

Another surprise was the number of hours we spent in that Land Cruiser. Most birding trips are brutal on the feet, requiring endless walking and standing. Because of the risk posed by African mammals, particularly elephants and buffalo, we were allowed out of the vehicle only at lodges and a few picnic areas. Even at the lodges where we could actually walk in forest, we had to bring along an armed guard and stick close together. This was hardest on my brother, who even as a two-year-old (you can see it in home movies) hated confinement and loved to wander by himself. Near the end of a hike at a small lodge near Ngorongoro, Tom was chafing so badly that I encouraged him to slip away and walk the last hundred yards by himself. For this, we received a severe lecture from our Rockjumper guide, David. Earlier in the trip, the other Tom had mentioned that his greatest fear was of being yelled at. After David's lecture, my brother admitted that this was his greatest fear, too.

Beyond surprises, the way a foreign reality gets through to you is by wearing you down. It took me a while, in Africa, to escape the feeling that I might as well have been in Florida. But eventually, because of the vastness of the parks of Tanzania and Kenya, and because of the overwhelming quantity of wildlife, I began to see the herds of herbivores as inhabitants of something resembling an intact ecosystem; to mentally place them within a historical continuum at whose earlier end they'd roamed freely all over the continent; and thus to connect, at least a little bit, with their amazingness.

I began to *see* them. There was the curious largeness of the zebras' heads, the sturdiness of their haunches as they scrambled up an incline; they looked eminently tameable and rideable, but apparently they're not, and this struck me as remarkable. The oryx—outstanding animals—had horns so long that they barely needed to turn their heads to scratch beneath their tails. The giraffes were so big that when they ran, as they sometimes did, they seemed to be galloping in slow motion. (This must be how our own movements appear to little birds.) The wildebeests were all about numbers: to see one in the Serengeti was to see a quarter million, and in migration they proceed single file, like an endless coal train in Montana, stretching from horizon to horizon. The hippopotamus is reputedly the most dangerous wild animal in Africa, but, for me, as I watched a large herd wallowing in a pond, blowing water at one another, rolling over to float with their pink bellies and circular soles pointing skyward, they were also the most endearing. For sheer charisma, however, nothing could top the buffalo. Their expressions were as badass as a Navy SEAL's, and there was a distinctly unbovine gleam of intelligence in their eyes. At Ngorongoro, we saw a giant bull taunting a trio of sleepy lions while the rest of his herd looked on raptly. Glancing over his shoulder, as if to assure himself of his audience, he advanced on the lions until they bestirred themselves, with gestures of annoyance, and found a different place to sleep. The bull then did a victory strut.

Having starred in so many films, the large cats were the hardest mammals to *see*. When we encountered fourteen lions sleeping in a tree, my main feeling was satisfaction in how ridiculous the biggest female looked, straddling a branch lengthwise, her hind legs dangling awkwardly. It was interesting to see a leopard walk headfirst down a perfectly vertical tree trunk, and to watch a caracal skin a rodent and consume it like a meat popsicle, in two bites. But the best cat moment, because it was the least expected—the rains had been late and heavy, and David had warned us that the grass was too tall to make a sighting likely—was of a female cheetah sitting up near the side of a road. She was gazing intently across the road, and twice, without breaking her gaze, she gave a sweet little bark. David pointed out a distant embankment where two cubs were peering back at her uncertainly, craning their necks. Who can resist the sight of worried cheetah cubs? I couldn't, for about five minutes. But then, as the cheetah show continued, the mother retrieving her cubs and leading them deeper into the grass, I began to scan the trees for birds.

The thing about birds is that no matter how well you've done your homework, no matter how carefully you've studied the expected species, it still feels like a surprise when you encounter one. In the Serengeti, we cruised one stretch of road repeatedly, hoping to find the Gray-crested Helmetshrike, a rare and localized species, to no avail. On our last afternoon, David and Geitan and I went out without the two Toms for one more try. David tried playing a recording of the helmetshrike's call, and immediately a tight flock of seven of them came swooping over to the road. Their grace and beauty were a welcome but unnecessary bonus. David and I high-fived while Geitan bounced in the driver's seat, silly with happiness, and pumped his ox-tail fly-swatter like a royal scepter, shouting, "We are heroes!"

The large iconic birds of East Africa—the ubiquitous Lilac-breasted Roller, the foppish Secretarybird, the gazelle-dwarfing Kori Bustard—can be enjoyed with the naked eye. Small posses of black-plumaged Ground Hornbills stroll placidly in the grass, surveying the scene with eyes so expressive they seem almost human, and then plunk themselves down to do some preening or maybe just to have a little think. Lappet-faced Vultures, the most massive avian scavengers, are the first to dine on the scraps of carrion gristle that hyenas have left behind; lesser vultures hang back, as if behind the rope outside a nightclub, and wait their turn; tall Marabou Storks stand by impassively, like tuxedoed waiters. Male ostriches doing their courtship display lurch and sway from side to side in a froth of white feathers. Although YouTube has videos of this spectacle, the full scale of it—an eight-foot-tall bird dancing like a very drunk male wedding guest—can be appreciated only in person.

But it was the smaller birds that brought me the deepest into Africa, by helping me forget I was a tourist. Whether a park is part of nature or merely a simulacrum is entirely in the eye of the human beholder. The animals themselves, large and small, are simply taking what they've been given and going about their lives as best they can. It's difficult, however, to admire a herd of elephants in the Serengeti without wondering if they've been driven into its confines by the pressure from ivory poachers and cattle farmers. To lose the postmodern context, to shrink your field of view, it helps to train your binoculars on something tiny.

In the breeding season, the male Long-tailed Widowbird grows a wide black tail nearly three times the length of its body—so long that, when it lands on a bush, it has to drape the tail over multiple branches, and when you watch it struggle to get airborne you can see the herculean straining of its wings. The weavers, a marvelous and gaudy family of birds endemic to Africa, hang their intricate spheroidal nests from slender tree branches, sometimes building false entryways to foil predators; to watch a brilliant orange-and-yellow weaver carry a blade of grass to the nest and deftly tuck it in among the other blades is to enter a world whose outer limits aren't much farther than a stone's throw away. The Flappet Lark, which gets my vote for the best East African bird name, is very hard to see outside its breeding season, when the male shoots up high into the air and hovers there, beating its wings so hard that it sounds like cards being shuffled. As long as the flapping noise lasts, you feel suspended in the air with it, and the patch of ground to which it then drops is a very specific place, the territory of one Flappet Lark.

You don't have to vacation in East Africa. You should do whatever you want. But, if you go, one way to make sure you've really been there is to bring some good binoculars. The most beautiful and moving thing I saw on my safari was a pair of Hunter's Cisticolas. As a family, the cisticolas are the drabbest of little beige birds. Many of the species are nearly impossible to tell apart unless you hear them sing; they're the kind of identification challenge that gives birding a bad name. But the pair I saw—saw well, with binoculars—was perched shoulder to shoulder on an acacia twig, facing in opposite directions, and singing a contrapuntal duet, their beaks open wide. Two melodies and one couple, singing of their coupledom. For a moment, their song and their twig were everything, because they were so small.

THE END OF THE END
OF THE EARTH

Two years ago, a lawyer in Indiana sent me a check for $78,000. The money was from my uncle Walt, who had died six months earlier. I hadn't been expecting any money from Walt, still less counting on it. So I thought I should earmark my inheritance for something special, to honor Walt's memory.

It happened that my longtime girlfriend, a native Californian, had promised to join me on a big vacation. She'd been feeling grateful to me for understanding why she had to return full-time to Santa Cruz and look after her mother, who was ninety-four and losing her short-term memory. She'd said to me, impulsively, "I will take a trip with you anywhere in the world you've always wanted to go." To this I'd replied, for reasons I'm at a loss to reconstruct, "Antarctica?" Her eyes widened in a way that I should have paid closer attention to. But a promise was a promise.

Hoping to make Antarctica more palatable to my temperate Californian, I decided to spend Walt's money on the most deluxe of bookings—a three-week Lindblad National Geographic expedition to Antarctica, South Georgia island, and the Falklands. I paid a deposit, and the Californian and I proceeded to joke, uneasily, when the topic arose, about the nasty cold weather and the heaving South Polar seas to which she'd consented to subject herself. I kept reassuring her that as soon as she saw a penguin she'd be happy she'd made the trip. But when it came time to pay the balance, she asked if we might postpone by a year. Her mother's situation was unstable, and she was loath to put herself so irretrievably far from home.

By this point, I, too, had developed a vague aversion to the trip, an inability to recall why I'd proposed Antarctica in the first place. The idea of "seeing it before it melts" was dismal and self-canceling: why not just wait for it to melt and cross *itself* off the list of travel destinations? I was also put off by the seventh continent's status as a trophy, too remote and expensive for the common tourist to set foot on. It was true that there were extraordinary birds to be seen, not just penguins but oddities like the Snowy Sheathbill and the world's southernmost-breeding songbird, the South Georgia Pipit. But the number of Antarctic species is fairly small, and I'd already reconciled myself to never seeing every bird species in the world. The best reason I could think of for going to Antarctica was that it was absolutely not the kind of thing the Californian and I did; we'd learned that our ideal getaway lasts three days. I thought that if she and I were at sea for three weeks, with no possibility of escape, we might discover new capacities in ourselves. We would do a thing together that we would then, for the rest of our lives, have done together.

And so I agreed to a year's postponement. I relocated to Santa Cruz myself. Then the Californian's mother had a worrisome fall, and the Californian became even more afraid of leaving her alone. Recognizing, finally, that it wasn't my job to make her life more difficult, I excused her from the trip. Luckily, my brother Tom, the only other person with whom I could imagine sharing a small cabin for three weeks, had just retired and was available to take her place. I changed the booking from a queen-size bed to twin beds, and I ordered insulated rubber boots and an exhaustively illustrated guide to Antarctic wildlife.

Even then, though, as the departure date approached, I couldn't bring myself to say that I was going to Antarctica. I kept saying, "It appears that I'm going to Antarctica." Tom reported being excited, but my own sense of unreality, of failure to pleasurably anticipate, grew only stronger. Maybe it was that Antarctica reminded me of death—the ecological death with which global warming is threatening it, or the deadline for seeing it that my own death represented. But I became acutely appreciative of the ordinary rhythm of life with the Californian, the sight of her face in the morning, the sound of the garage door when she returned from her evening visit to her mother. When I packed my suitcase, it was as if I were doing the bidding of the money I'd paid.

In St. Louis, in August 1976, on an evening cool enough that my parents and I were eating dinner on the porch, my mother got up to answer the phone in the kitchen and immediately summoned my father. "It's Irma," she said. Irma was my father's sister, who lived with Walt in Dover, Delaware. It must have been clear that something terrible had happened, because I remember being in the kitchen, standing near my mother, when my father interrupted whatever Irma was saying to him and shouted into the telephone, as if in anger, *Irma, my God, is she dead?*

Irma and Walt were my godparents, but I didn't know them well. My mother couldn't stand Irma—she maintained that Irma had been terminally spoiled by her parents, at my father's expense—and although Walt was felt to be much the more lik-able of the two, a retired Air Force colonel who'd become a high-school guidance counselor, I knew him mainly from a self-published volume of golf wisdom that he'd sent us, *Eclectic Golf,* which, because I read everything, I'd read. The person I'd seen more of was Walt and Irma's only child, Gail. She was a tall and pretty and adventurous young woman who'd gone to college in Missouri and often stopped to see us. She'd graduated the pre-vious year and had taken a job as a silversmith's apprentice at Colonial Williamsburg, in Virginia. What Irma was calling to tell us was that Gail, while driving alone, overnight, in heavy rain, to a rock concert in Ohio, had lost control of her car on one of West Virginia's narrow, winding highways. Although Irma apparently couldn't bring herself to say the words, Gail was dead.

I was sixteen and understood what death was. And yet, per-haps because my parents didn't bring me along to the funeral, I didn't cry or grieve for Gail. What I had, instead, was a feeling that her death was somehow inside my head—as if my network of memories of her had been cauterized by some hideous needle and now constituted a zone of nullity, a zone of essential, bad truth. The zone was too forbidding to enter consciously, but I could sense it there, behind a mental cordon, the irreversibility of my lovely cousin's death.

A year and a half after the accident, when I was a college freshman in Pennsylvania, my mother conveyed to me an invi-tation from Irma and Walt to come to Dover for a weekend, along with her own strict instruction that I say yes. In my imagination, the house in Dover was an embodiment of the zone of bad truth in my head. I went there with a dread which the house proceeded to justify. It had the uncluttered, oppressively clean formality of an official residence. The floor-length curtains, their stiffness, the precision of their folds, seemed to say that no breath or movement of Gail's would ever stir them. My aunt's hair was pure white and looked as stiff as the curtains. The whiteness of her face was intensified by crimson lipstick and heavy eyeliner.

I learned that only my parents called Irma Irma; to everyone else, she was Fran, a shortening of her maiden name. I'd dreaded a scene of open grief, but Fran filled the minutes and the hours by talking to me incessantly, in a strained and overloud voice. The talk—about her house's decor, about her acquaintance with Delaware's governor, about the direction the nation had taken—was exquisitely boring in its remoteness from ordinary feeling. By and by, she spoke of Gail in the same way: the essential nature of Gail's personality, the quality of Gail's artistic talents, the high idealism of Gail's plans for the future. I said very little, as did Walt. My aunt's droning was unbearable, but I may already have understood that the zone she was inhabiting was itself unbearable, and that talking loftily about nothing, nonstop, was how a person might survive in it; how, indeed, she might enable a visitor to survive in it. Basically, I saw that Fran was adaptively out of her mind. My only respite from her that weekend was the auto tour Walt gave me of Dover and its Air Force base. Walt was a lean, tall man, ethnically Slovenian, with a beak of a nose and hair persisting only behind his ears. His nickname was Baldy.

I visited him and Fran twice more while I was in college, and they came to my graduation and to my wedding, and then, for many years, I had little contact with them beyond birthday cards and my mother's reporting (always colored by her dislike of Fran) on the dutiful stops that she and my father made in Boynton Beach, Florida, where Fran and Walt had moved into a golf-centered condominium complex. But then, after my father died, and while my mother was losing her battle with cancer, a funny thing happened: Walt became smitten with my mother.

Fran by now was straightforwardly demented, with Alzheimer's, and had entered a nursing home. Since my father had also had Alzheimer's, Walt had reached out by telephone to my mother for advice and commiseration. According to her, he'd then traveled by himself to St. Louis, where the two of them, finding themselves alone together for the first time, had uncovered so much common ground—each was an optimistic lover of life, long married to a rigid and depressive Franzen—that they'd fallen into a dizzying kind of ease with each other, an incipiently romantic intimacy. Walt had taken her downtown to her favorite restaurant, and afterward, at the wheel of her car, he'd scraped a fender on the wall of a parking garage; the two of them, giggling, a little bit drunk, had agreed to split the repair cost and tell no one. (Walt did eventually tell me.) Soon after his visit, my mother's health worsened, and she went to Seattle to spend her remaining days in my brother Tom's house. But Walt made plans to come and see her and continue what they'd started. Of the feelings they had for each other, his were still forward-looking. Hers were more bittersweet, the sadness of opportunities she knew she'd missed.

It was my mother who opened my eyes to what a gem Walt was, and it was Walt's dismay and sorrow, after she'd died suddenly, before he could see her again, that opened the door to my friendship with him. He needed someone to know that he'd begun to fall in love with her, the joyous surprise of that, and to appreciate how keenly he therefore felt the loss of her. Because I, too, in the last few years of my mother's life, had experienced a surprising upsurge of admiration and affection for her, and because I had a lot of time on my hands—I was childless, divorced, underemployed, and now parentless—I became the person Walt could talk to.

During my first visit to him, a few months after my mother died, we did the essential South Florida things: nine holes of golf at his condominium complex, two rubbers of bridge with two friends in their nineties in Delray Beach, and a stop at the nursing home where my aunt dwelled. We found her lying in bed in a tight fetal position. Walt tenderly fed her a dish of ice cream and a dish of pudding. When a nurse came in to change a Band-Aid on her hip, Fran burst into tears, her face contorting like a baby's, and wailed that it hurt, it hurt, it was horrible, it wasn't fair.

We left her with the nurse and returned to his apartment. Many of Fran's formal furnishings had come along from Dover, but now a bachelor scattering of magazines and cereal boxes had loosened their death grip. Walt spoke to me with plain emotion about the loss of Gail and the question of her old belongings. Would I like to have some of her drawings? Would I take the Pentax SLR he'd given her? The drawings had the look of school projects, and I didn't need a camera, but I sensed that Walt was looking for a way to disencumber himself of things he couldn't bear to simply donate to Goodwill. I said I'd be very happy to take them.

In Santiago, the night before our charter flight to the southern tip of Argentina, Tom and I attended Lindblad's welcoming reception in a Ritz-Carlton function room. Because berths on our ship, the *National Geographic Orion*, started at $22,000 and went up to almost double that, I'd pre-stereotyped my fellow passengers as plutocratic nature lovers—leather-skinned retirees with trophy spouses and tax-haven home addresses, maybe a face or two I recognized from television. But I'd done the math wrong. There turn out to be special yachts for that clientele. The crowd in the function room was less glamorous than I'd expected, and less octogenarian. A plurality of the hundred of us were merely physicians or attorneys, and I could see only one man in pants hiked up around his stomach.

My third-biggest fear about the expedition, after seasickness and disturbing my brother with my snoring, was that insufficient diligence would be devoted to finding the bird species unique to the Antarctic. After a Lindblad staffer, an Australian whose luggage for the trip had been lost by his airline, had greeted us and taken some questions from the crowd, I raised my hand and said I was a birder and asked who else was. I was hoping to establish the existence of a powerful constituency, but I saw only two hands go up. The Australian, who'd praised each of the earlier questions as "excellent," did not praise mine. He said, rather vaguely, that there would be staff members on the ship who knew their birds.

I soon learned that the two raised hands had belonged to the only two passengers who hadn't paid full fare. They were a conservationist couple in their fifties, Chris and Ada, from Mount Shasta, California. Ada had a sister who worked for Lindblad, and they'd been offered a slashed-rate stateroom ten days before departure, owing to a cancellation. This added to my feeling of kinship with them. Although I could afford to pay full fare, I wouldn't have chosen a cruise line like Lindblad for my own sake; I'd done it for the Californian, to soften the blow of Antarctica, and was feeling like an accidental luxury tourist myself.

The next day, at the airport in Ushuaia, Argentina, Tom and

I found ourselves near the rear of a slow line for passport control. At the urgent instruction of Lindblad, before leaving home, I'd paid the "reciprocity fee" that Argentina charged American tourists, but Tom had been in Argentina three years earlier. The government's website hadn't let him pay his fee again, so he'd printed a copy of its refusal and taken it with him, figuring that the printout, plus the Argentine stamps in his passport, would get him over the border. They didn't get him over the border. While the other Lindblad passengers boarded the buses that were taking us to a lunchtime cruise on a catamaran, we stood and pleaded with an immigration officer. Half an hour passed. A further twenty minutes passed. The Lindblad handlers were tearing their hair. Finally, when it looked as if Tom would be allowed to pay his fee a second time, I ran outside and boarded a bus and charged into a sea of dirty looks. The trip hadn't even started, and Tom and I were already the problem passengers.

On board the *Orion*, our expedition leader, Doug, summoned everyone to the ship's lounge and greeted us energetically. Doug was burly and white-bearded, a former theatrical designer. "I *love* this trip!" he said into his microphone. "This is the greatest trip, by the greatest company, to the greatest destination in the world. I'm at least as excited as any of you are." The trip, he hastened to add, was not a cruise. It was an expedition, and he wanted us to know that he was the kind of expedition leader who, if he and the captain spied the right opportunity, would *tear up the plan*, throw it out the window, and *go chase great adventure*.

Throughout the trip, Doug continued, two staffers would give photography lessons and work individually with passengers who wanted to improve their images. Two other staffers would go diving wherever possible, to supply us with additional images. The Australian who'd lost his luggage had not lost the late-model drone, with a high-definition video camera, that he'd worked for nine months to get the permits to use on our trip. The drone would be supplying images, too. And then there was the full-time videographer, who would create a DVD that we could all buy at trip's end. I got the impression that other people in the lounge had a clearer grasp than I of the point of coming to Antarctica. Evidently, the point was to bring home images. The National Geographic brand had led me to expect science where I should have been thinking of pictures. My sense of being a problem passenger deepened.

In the days that followed, I was taught what to ask when you meet a person on a Lindblad ship: "Is this your first Lindblad?" Or, alternately, "Have you done a Lindblad before?" I found these locutions unsettling, as if "a Lindblad" were something vaguely but expensively spiritual. Doug typically began his evening recap, in the lounge, by asking, "Was this a great day or was this a great day?" and then waiting for a cheer. He made sure we knew that we'd been specially blessed by a smooth crossing of the Drake Passage, which had saved us enough time to land in our Zodiac dinghies on Barrientos Island, near the Antarctic Peninsula. This was a very special landing, not something every Lindblad expedition got to do.

It was late in the nesting season for the Gentoo and Chinstrap Penguins on Barrientos. Some of the chicks had fledged and followed their parents back into the sea, which is the preferred element of penguins and their only source of food. But thousands of birds remained. Fluffy gray chicks chased after any adult that was plausibly their parent, begging for a regurgitated meal, or banded together for safety from the gull-like skuas that preyed on the orphaned and the failing-to-thrive. Many of the adults had retreated uphill to molt, a process that involves standing still for several weeks, itchy and hungry, while new feathers push out old feathers. The patience of the molters, their silent endurance, was impossible not to admire in human terms. Although the colony was everywhere smeared with nitric-smelling shit, and the doomed orphan chicks were a piteous sight, I was already glad I'd come.

The scopolamine patches that Tom and I were wearing on our necks had dispelled my two biggest fears. With the help of the patch and calm waters, I wasn't getting seasick, and, with the help of the snore-muffling noise that we blasted on our clock radio, Tom was getting ten hours of deep scopolamine sleep every night. My third fear, however, had been on target. At no point did a Lindblad naturalist join Chris and Ada and me to watch seabirds from the observation deck. There wasn't even a good field guide to Antarctic wildlife in the *Orion*'s library. Instead, there were dozens of books about South Polar explorers, notably Ernest Shackleton—a figure scarcely less fetishized on board than the Lindblad experience itself. Sewn onto the left sleeve of my company-issued orange parka was a badge with Shackleton's portrait, commemorating the centennial of his epic open-boat voyage from Elephant Island. We were given a book about Shackleton, PowerPoint lectures about Shackleton, special tours to Shackleton-related sites, a screening of a long film about a re-creation of Shackleton's voyage, and a chance to hike three miles of the arduous trail that Shackleton had survived at the end of it. (Late in the trip, under the gaze of our videographer, we would all be herded to the grave of Shackleton, handed shot glasses of Irish whiskey, and invited to join in a toast to him.) The message seemed to be that we, on our Lindblad, were not un-Shackletonian ourselves. Failing to feel heroic on the *Orion* was a recipe for loneliness. I was grateful that I at least had two compatriots with whom to study the wildlife guides we'd brought, and to puzzle out the field marks of the Antarctic Prion (a small seabird), and to try to discern the species-distinguishing hue of the bill of a fast-flying giant petrel.

As we progressed down the peninsula, Doug began dangling the possibility of exciting news. Finally, he gathered us in the lounge and revealed that it was actually happening: because of favorable winds, he and the captain had *thrown out the plan*. We had a very special opportunity to cross below the Antarctic Circle, and would now be steaming hard to the south.

The night before we reached the circle, Doug warned us that he might come on the intercom fairly early in the morning to wake those passengers who wanted to look outside and see the "magenta line" (he was joking) as we crossed it. And wake us he did, at six thirty, with another joke about the magenta line. As the ship bore down on it, Doug dramatically counted down from five. Then he congratulated "every person on board," and Tom and I went back to sleep. Only later did we learn that the *Orion* had approached the Antarctic Circle much earlier than six thirty—at an hour when a person hesitates to wake up millionaires, an hour too dark for taking a picture. Chris, it turned out, had been awake before dawn and had followed the ship's coordinates on his cabin's TV screen. He'd watched as the ship slowed down, tacked west, and then executed a fishhook turn and steamed due north to buy time.

Although Doug came off as the chief simulacrum manager for a brand with cultish aspects, I had sympathy for him. He was finishing his first season as a Lindblad expedition leader, was clearly exhausted, and was under intense pressure to deliver the trip of a lifetime to customers who, not being plutocrats after all, expected value for their money. Doug was also, as far as I could determine, the only person on the ship besides me who'd been a birder serious enough to keep a list of the species he'd seen. He'd given up listing, but in one of his nightly recaps he told the amusing story of his desperation and failure to find a pipit on his first trip to South Georgia. If he hadn't been frantically catering to a shipful of image seekers, I would have liked to get to know him.

It should also be said that Antarctica lived up to Doug's enthusiasm. I'd never before had the experience of beholding scenic beauty so dazzling that I couldn't process it, couldn't get it to register as something real that I was really in the presence of. A trip that had seemed unreal to me beforehand had taken me to a place that likewise seemed unreal, albeit in a better way. Global warming may be endangering the continent's western ice sheet, but Antarctica is still far from having melted. On either side of the Lemaire Channel were spiky black mountains, extremely tall but still not so tall as to be merely snow-covered; they were *buried* in wind-carved snowdrift, all the way to their peaks, with rock exposed only on the most vertical cliffs. Sheltered from wind, the water was glassy, and under a solidly gray sky it was absolutely black, pristinely black, like outer space. Amid the monochromes, the endless black and white and gray, was the jarring blue of glacial ice. No matter the shade of it—the bluish tinge of the growlers bobbing in our wake, the intensely deep blue of the arched and chambered floating ice castles, the Styrofoamish powder blue of calving glaciers—I couldn't make my eyes believe that they were seeing a color from nature. Again and again, I nearly laughed in disbelief. Immanuel Kant had defined the Sublime as beauty plus terror, but as I experienced it in Antarctica, from the safe vantage of a ship with a glass-and-brass elevator and first-rate espresso, it was more like a mixture of beauty and absurdity.

The *Orion* sailed on through eerily glassy seas. Nothing man-made could be seen on land or ice or water, no building or other ship, and up on the forward observation deck the *Orion*'s engines were inaudible. Standing there in the silence with Chris and Ada, scanning for petrels, I felt as if we were alone in the world and being pulled forward toward the end of it, like the *Dawn Treader* in Narnia, by some irresistible invisible current. But when we entered an area of pack ice and became surrounded by it, images were needed. A Zodiac was noisily launched, the Australian's drone unleashed.

Late in the day, in Lallemand Fjord, near the southernmost latitude we reached, Doug announced another "operation." The captain would ram the ship into the huge ice field at the head of the fjord, and we could then choose between paddling around in sea kayaks or taking a walk on the ice. I knew that the fjord was our last hope for seeing an Emperor Penguin; seven other penguin species were likely on the trip, but the Emperors rarely venture north of the Antarctic Circle. While the rest of the passengers hurried to their rooms to put on their life jackets and adventure boots, I set up a telescope on the observation deck. Scanning the ice field, which was dotted with crabeater seals and small Adélie Penguins, I immediately caught a glimpse of a bird that looked unfamiliar. It seemed to have a patch of color behind its ear and a blush of yellow on its breast. *Emperor Penguin?* The magnified image was dim and unsteady, and most of the bird's body was hidden by a little iceberg, and either the ship or the iceberg was drifting. Before I could get a proper look, the iceberg had obscured the bird altogether.

What to do? Emperor Penguins may be the world's greatest bird. Four feet tall, the stars of *March of the Penguins*, they incubate their eggs in the Antarctic winter as far as a hundred miles from the sea, the males huddling together for warmth, the females waddling or tobogganing to open water for food, every one of them as heroic as Shackleton. But the bird I'd glimpsed was easily half a mile away, and I was aware of being a problem passenger who'd already been involved in one lengthy delay of the group. I was also aware of my distressing history of incorrect bird identifications. What were the chances of randomly pointing a scope at the ice and instantly spotting the most sought-after species of the trip? I didn't feel as if I'd *made up* the yellow blush and the patch of color. But sometimes the birder's eye sees what it hopes to see.

After an existentialist moment, conscious of deciding my fate, I ran down to the bridge deck and found my favorite staff naturalist hurrying in the direction of Doug's operation. I grabbed his sleeve and said I thought I'd seen an Emperor Penguin.

"An Emperor? You sure?"

"Ninety percent sure."

"We'll check it out," he said, pulling away from me.

He didn't sound like he meant it, so I ran down to Chris and Ada's cabin, banged on their door, and gave them my news. God bless them for believing it. They took off their life jackets and followed me back up to the observation deck. By now, unfortunately, I'd lost track of the penguin spot; there were so many little icebergs. I went down to the bridge itself, where a different staffer, a Dutch woman, gave me a more satisfactory response: "Emperor Penguin! That's a key species for us, we have to tell the captain right away."

Captain Graser was a skinny, peppy German probably older than he looked. He wanted to know exactly where the bird was. I pointed at my best guess, and he got on the radio with Doug and told him that we had to move the ship. I could hear Doug's exasperation on the radio. He was in the middle of an operation! The captain instructed him to suspend it.

As the ship began to move, and I considered how annoyed Doug would be if I'd been wrong about the bird, I rediscovered the little iceberg. Chris and Ada and I stood at the rail and watched it through our binoculars. But there was nothing behind it now, at least nothing that we could see before the ship stopped and turned around. Radios were squawking impatiently. After the captain had rammed us into the ice, Chris spotted a promising bird that quickly dived into the water. But then Ada thought she saw it come flopping back onto the ice. Chris put the scope on it, had a long look, and turned to me with a deadpan expression. "I concur," he said.

We high-fived. I fetched Captain Graser, who took one look through the scope and let out a whoop. "Ja, ja," he said, "Emperor Penguin! Emperor Penguin! Just like I was hoping!" He said he'd trusted my report because, on a previous trip, he'd seen a lone Emperor in the same area. Emitting further whoops, he danced a jig, an actual jig, and then hurried off to the Zodiacs to have a closer look.

The Emperor he'd seen earlier had been exceptionally friendly or inquisitive, and it appeared that I'd refound the same bird, because as soon as the captain approached it we saw it flop down on its belly and toboggan toward him eagerly. Doug, on the intercom, announced that the captain had made an exciting discovery and the plan had changed. Hikers already on the ice bent their steps toward the bird, the rest of us piled into Zodiacs. By the time I arrived on the scene, thirty orange-jacketed photographers were standing or kneeling and training their lenses on a very tall and very handsome penguin, very close to them.

I'd already made a quiet, alienated resolution not to take a single picture on the trip. And here was an image so indelible that no camera was needed to capture it: the Emperor Penguin appeared to be holding a press conference. While a cluster of Adélies came up from behind it, observing like support staff, the Emperor faced the press corps in a posture of calm dignity. After a while, it gave its neck a leisurely stretch. Demonstrating its masterly balance and flexibility, and yet without seeming to show off, it scratched behind its ear with one foot while standing fully erect on the other. And then, as if to underline how comfortable it felt with us, it fell asleep.

At the following evening's recap, Captain Graser warmly thanked the birders. He'd reserved a special table for us in the dining room, with free wine on offer. A card on the table read KING EMPEROR. Ordinarily, the ship's waiters, who were mostly Filipino, addressed Tom as Sir Tom and me as Sir Jon, which made me feel like John Falstaff. But that evening I really was feeling like King Emperor. All day long, passengers I hadn't even met had stopped me in hallways to thank me or cheer me for finding the penguin. I finally had an inkling of how it must feel to be a high-school athlete and come to school after scoring a season-saving touchdown. For forty years, in large social groups, I'd accustomed myself to feeling like the problem. To be a group's game-winning hero, if only for a day, was a complete, disorienting novelty. I wondered if, all my life, in my refusal to be a joiner, I'd missed out on some essential human thing.

My uncle, the Air Force veteran, now buried in the ranks at Arlington, was a lifelong joiner. Walt never ceased to be passionately loyal to his hometown of Chisholm, in Minnesota's Iron

Range, where he'd grown up without much money. He'd been a college hockey player and then a bomber pilot in the Second World War, flying thirty-five missions in North Africa and South Asia. He was a self-taught pianist, able to play any standard by ear; the elements of his golf swing were eclectic. He wrote two memoirs devoted to the many great friends he'd made in life. He was also a liberal Democrat who'd married a stringent Republican. He could strike up a lively conversation with almost anyone, and I could imagine the unfettered fun that my mother could imagine having had if she'd been with a regular guy like Walt and not my father.

One night, at the restaurant in the South Florida condominium complex, over several cocktails, Walt told me the story not only of him and my mother but of him and Fran and Gail. After retiring from combat, he said, and after leading an officer's social life with Fran at various overseas bases, he'd realized that he'd made a mistake in marrying her. It wasn't just that her parents had spoiled her; she was an implacable social striver who hated and denied her backwoods Minnesota background as much as he loved and celebrated his own; she was unbearable. "I was weak," he said. "I should have left her, but I was weak."

They had their only child when Fran was in her mid-thirties, and Fran quickly became so obsessed with Gail, and so averse to sex with Walt, that he felt driven to seek comfort elsewhere. "There were other women," he told me. "I had affairs. But I always made it clear that I was a family man and wasn't leaving Fran. On Sundays, my buddies and I would get loaded up on liquor and drive over to Baltimore to watch Johnny Unitas and the Colts." At home, Fran grew ever more micromanagerial in her attention to Gail's personal appearance, to her schoolwork, to her art projects. Gail seemed to be all Fran could talk about or think about. Four years at college had brought some relief, but as soon as Gail returned to the East Coast, and went to work in Williamsburg, Fran redoubled her intrusions into her daughter's life.

Walt could see that something was terribly wrong; that Gail was being driven crazy by her mother but didn't know how to escape. By early August 1976, he'd become so desperate that he did the only thing he could do. He announced to Fran that he was going back to Minnesota, back to his beloved Chisholm, and that he wasn't going to live with her again—couldn't be married to her—unless she curtailed her obsession with their daughter. Then he packed a bag and drove to Minnesota. He was there, in Chisholm, ten days later, when Gail set out to drive through the night in bad weather across West Virginia. Gail was aware, he said, that he'd made a break with her mother. He'd told her himself.

Walt ended his story there, and we spoke of other things—his wish to find a girlfriend among the other residents of the complex, his clearness of conscience regarding this wish, now that my mother was dead and Fran was in a nursing home, and his worry that he was too much of a country boy, too unpolished, for the stylish widows at the complex. I wondered if he'd omitted the coda to his story because it went without saying: how, after an accident in West Virginia that could never be untangled from his flight to Minnesota, and after Fran had lost the one person in the world who mattered to her, becoming locked forever in brittle posthumous monomania, a world of pain, he'd had no choice but to return to her and devote himself henceforth to caring for her.

I saw that Gail's death hadn't merely been "tragic" in the hackneyed sense. It had partaken of the irony and inevitability of dramatic tragedy, compounded by the twenty-plus years that Walt had then devoted to listening to Fran, leavened only by the tenderness of his solicitude toward her. He really was a nice guy. He had a heart full of love and had given it to his broken wife, and I was moved not only by the tragedy but by the ordinary humanity of the man at the center of it. I had a sense of astonishment as well. Concealed in plain sight, my whole life, amid the moral rigidity and Swedish standoffishness of my father's family, had been a regular guy who had affairs and drove to Baltimore with his buddies and manfully accepted his fate. I wondered if my mother had seen in him what I'd now seen, and had loved him for it, as I now did.

The following afternoon, Walt's friend Ed called and asked him to come to his house with jumper cables. Arriving at the house, we found Ed standing in the street beside an enormous American car. Ed looked nearly dead—his skin was a terrible yellow and he was swaying on his feet. He said he'd been sick for a month and was feeling much better. But when Walt connected the jumper cables to Ed's car and asked him to try turning over the engine, Ed reminded him that he was too weak to turn the ignition key. (He had, however, been hoping to drive the car.) I got into Ed's car myself. As soon as I tried the key, I could tell that the car's problem was worse than a dead battery. Ed's car was utterly nonresponsive, and I said so. But Walt wasn't happy with how the jumper cables were connected. He backed his own car away, dragging a cable and snagging it on the pavement. Before I could stop him, he'd torn off the cable's gripper, and the person he became upset with was me. I worked to reattach the gripper with a screwdriver, but he didn't like how I was doing it. He tried to grab it away from me, and he barked at me, shouted at me. "God damn it, Jonathan! God *damn* it! That's not right!

Give it here! God damn it!" Ed, now sitting in the passenger seat, had slumped sideways and was listing downward. Walt and I tussled over the screwdriver, which I wouldn't let go of; I was angry at him, too. When we'd calmed down, and I'd repaired the cable to his satisfaction, I turned the key of Ed's car again. The car was nonresponsive.

After that first visit, I tried to get to Florida every year to see Walt, and to call him every few months. He did eventually find a girlfriend, a sterling one. Even when his hearing worsened and his mind began to cloud, I could sustain a conversation with him. We continued to have moments of intensity, like the time he told me how important it was to him that I someday tell his story, and I promised that I would. But it seems to me that we were never closer than the day he'd shouted at me about the jumper cable. There was something uncanny about that shouting. It was as if he'd forgotten—had been made to forget, perhaps by the overt mortality of Ed and his car, perhaps by the refraction of his love for my mother through the person of me—that he and I didn't have a real history together; had spent, in our lives, no more than a cumulative week with each other. He'd shouted at me the way a father might have shouted at a son.

The Californian had been right to fear the weather, which was colder than I'd led her to believe. But I'd been right about the penguins. From the Antarctic Peninsula, where their numbers were impressive, the *Orion*'s route took us north again and then far east, to South Georgia island, where their numbers were staggering. South Georgia is a principal breeding site for the King Penguin, a species nearly as tall as the Emperor and even more dramatically plumaged. To see a King Penguin in the wild seemed to me, in itself, sufficient reason not only to have made the journey; it seemed reason enough to have been born on this planet. Admittedly, I love birds. But I believe that a visitor from any other planet, observing a King Penguin alongside even the most perfect human specimen, with vision unclouded by the possibility of sexual attraction, would declare the penguin the obviously more beautiful species. And it's not just the hypothetical extraterrestrial. Everybody loves penguins. In the erectness of their bearing, and in their readiness to drop down on their bellies, the flinging way they gesture with their armlike flippers, the shortness of the strides with which they walk or boldly scamper on their fleshy feet, they resemble human children more closely than does any other animal, not excepting the great apes.

Having evolved on remote coastlines, Antarctic penguins are also the rare animal with absolutely no fear of us. When I sat on the ground, the King Penguins came so close to me that I could have stroked their gleaming, furlike feathers. Their plumage had the hypercrispness of pattern, the hypervividness of color, that you can normally experience only by taking drugs. The colonies of Gentoos and Chinstraps had not been great for sitting down, because of the excrement. But the King Penguins were, as one Lindblad naturalist put it, more tidy. At Saint Andrews Bay, on South Georgia, where half a million adult kings and downy king chicks were gathered tightly together, all I smelled was sea and alpine air.

Though every penguin species has its charms—the glam-rock head streamers of the Macaroni Penguin, the little parallel-footed jumps with which a Rockhopper patiently climbs or descends a steep slope—I loved the Kings above all others. They combined untoppable aesthetic splendor with the intently social energies of children at play. After porpoising toward shore, a group of Kings would come running headlong up from the breakers, their flippers outstretched and fluttering, as if the water had gotten too cold for them. Or a lone bird would stand in shallow surf and gaze out to sea for so long that you wondered what thought was in its head. Or a pair of young males, excitedly tottering after an undecided female, would pause to see which of them was the more impressive craner of its neck, or to whap at each other ineffectually with their flippers. They had viciously sharp bills but sparred instead with punchless wings.

At Saint Andrews, the activity was mostly on the outskirts of the colony. Because so many of the birds were incubating eggs or molting, the main colony itself seemed strikingly peaceful. The view of it from above reminded me of Los Angeles as seen from Griffith Park very early on a weekend morning. A drowsy megalopolis of upright penguins. Patroling the thoroughfares were the sheathbills, strange snow-white birds with the body of a pigeon and the habits of a vulture. Even the amazing sound the Kings made—a spiraling festive bray that was sort of like bagpipes, sort of like a holiday noisemaker, and sort of like the "woofing dog" sound on certain airplanes, but really like nothing on earth I'd ever heard—had a soothing effect when thousands of distant penguins were making it together.

In the twentieth century, human beings did penguins a favor by all but extirpating many of the whales and seals that they competed with for food. Penguin populations rose, and South Georgia has lately become even more hospitable to them, because the rapid retreat of its glaciers is exposing land suitable for nesting. But humanity's benefit to penguins may be short-lived. If climate change continues to acidify the oceans, the water will reach a pH at which ocean invertebrates can't grow their shells; one of these invertebrates, krill, is a dietary staple of many penguin species. Climate change is also rapidly diminishing the Antarctic Peninsula's encircling ice, which provides a platform for the algae on which krill feed in winter, and which has hitherto protected krill from large-scale commercial exploitation. Supertanker-size factory ships may soon be coming from China, from Norway, from South Korea, to vacuum up the food on which not only the penguins but many whales and seals depend.

Krill are pinkie-size, pinkie-colored crustaceans. Estimating the total amount of them in the Antarctic is difficult, but a frequently cited figure, five hundred million metric tons, could make the species the world's largest repository of animal biomass. Unfortunately for penguins, many countries consider krill good eating, both for humans (the taste is said to be acquirable) and especially for farm fish and livestock. Currently, the total reported annual take of krill is less than half a million tons, with Norway leading the list of harvesters. China, however, has announced its intention to increase its harvest to as much as two million tons a year, and has begun building the ships needed to do it. As the chairman of China's National Agricultural Development Group has explained, "Krill provides very good quality protein that can be processed into food and medicine. The Antarctic is a treasure house for all human beings, and China should go there and share."

The Antarctic marine ecosystem is indeed the richest in the world; it's also the last remaining substantially intact one. Commercial use of it is monitored and regulated, at least nominally, by the Commission for the Conservation of Antarctic Marine Living Resources. But decisions by the commission may be vetoed by any of its twenty-five members, and one of them, China, has a history of resisting the designation of some large marine protected areas. Another, Russia, has lately become openly in-transigent, not only vetoing the establishment of new protected areas but questioning the very authority of the convention to establish them. Thus the future of krill, and with it the future of many penguin species, depends on uncertainties multiplied by uncertainties: how much krill there really is, how resiliently it can respond to climate change, whether any of it can now be harvested without starving other wildlife, whether such a harvest can even be regulated, and whether international cooperation on Antarctica can withstand new geopolitical conflicts. What isn't uncertain is that global temperatures, global population, and global demand for animal protein are all rising fast.

Mealtimes on the *Orion* inevitably put me in mind of the sanatorium in *The Magic Mountain*: the thrice-daily rush for the dining room, the hermetic isolation from the world, the unchanging faces at the tables. Instead of Frau Stöhr, dropping the name of Beethoven's "Erotica," there was the Donald Trump supporter and his wife. There was the merry alcoholic couple. There was the Dutch rheumatologist, her rheumatologist second husband, her rheumatologist daughter, and the daughter's rheumatologist boyfriend. There was the pair of couples who, whenever the Zodiacs were being loaded, jostled their way to the front of the line. There was the man who, by special permission, had brought along ham-radio equipment and was spending his vacation in the ship's library, trying to contact fellow hobbyists. There were the Australians who mostly didn't mix.

By way of mealtime small talk, I asked people why they'd come to Antarctica. I learned that many were simply devotees of

Lindblad. Some had heard, while on a different Lindblad, that a Lindblad to Antarctica was the best Lindblad, possibly excepting a Sea of Cortez Lindblad. One couple whom I liked very much, a doctor and a nurse, Bob and Gigi, had come to celebrate their twenty-fifth anniversary one year late. Another man, a retired chemist, told me that he'd chosen Antarctica only because he'd run out of other places he hadn't been. I was glad that nobody mentioned seeing Antarctica before it melts. The surprise was that, for nearly the entire trip, not one staff person or passenger even uttered the words *climate change* in my hearing.

Granted, I was skipping many of the onboard lectures. To prove myself a hardest-core birder, I needed to be up on the observation deck. The hardest-core birder stands all day in biting wind and salt spray, staring into fog or glare in the hope of glimpsing something unusual. Even when your intuition is telling you that nothing's out there, the only way to know for sure is to put in the hours and examine every speck of birdlife out to the horizon, every Antarctic Prion (might be a rare and exciting Fairy Prion) darting among waves whose color it matches exactly, every Wandering Albatross (might be a Royal Albatross) deciding whether the ship's wake is worth following. Seawatching is sometimes nauseating, often freezing, and almost always punishingly dull. After I'd racked up thirty hours of it and tallied exactly one seabird of note, a Kerguelen Petrel, I dialed back and devoted myself to the more sociable compulsion of playing bridge.

The other players, Diana and Nancy and Jacq, came from Seattle and belonged to a book club that had several other members on the ship. Along with Chris and Ada, they became my friends. In one of the early hands we played, I made a stupid discard, and Diana, a formidable bankruptcy attorney, laughed at me and said, "That was a *terrible* play." I liked her for this. I liked the foulness of the language at the table. When my partner, Nancy, who owns a forklift dealership, was playing her first slam contract of the trip, and I'd pointed out that the rest of the tricks were hers, she snapped at me, "Let me play the cards, you shit." She told me she'd meant it affectionately. The third player, Jacq, also an attorney, told me that she'd written a stage play about a Thanksgiving dinner she'd attended at Diana's, in the course of which Diana's ailing husband had died in bed in the family room. Jacq had the only tattoo I noticed on any passenger.

As in *The Magic Mountain*, the early days of the expedition were long and memorable, the later ones more of an accelerating blur. As soon as I'd had a rewarding encounter with South Georgia Pipits (they were gorgeous and confiding), I lost interest in visiting abandoned whaling stations. Even in Doug's voice, on our fifth day at South Georgia, a weariness was audible when he said, "So I think we'll do another sea kayak." He sounded like Vladimir and Estragon when they decide, late in *Godot*, after exhausting every other conceivable distraction, to "do the tree."

Toward the end of the trip's final day, which I'd mostly spent at the bridge table while hundreds of potentially interesting seabirds wheeled around outside, I went down to the lounge for a lecture on climate change. The lecture was delivered by the drone-flying Australian, whose name is Adam, and was attended by fewer than half the passengers. I wondered why Lindblad had postponed such an important lecture until the last day. The charitable explanation was that Lindblad, which prides itself on its environmental consciousness, wanted to send us home fired up to do more to protect the natural grandeur we'd enjoyed.

Adam's opening plea to us suggested other explanations. "Passenger-comment cards," he said, "are not the place to voice your beliefs about climate change." He laughed uneasily. "Don't shoot the messenger." He proceeded to ask how many of us believed the Earth's climate was changing. Everyone in the lounge raised a hand. And how many of us believed that human activity was causing it? Again, most hands were raised, but not the Donald Trump supporter's, not the ham hobbyist's. From the very back of the lounge came the curmudgeonly voice of Chris: "What about the people who think it isn't a matter of belief?"

"Excellent question," Adam said.

His lecture was a barn-burning reprise of *An Inconvenient Truth*, including the famous "hockey stick" graph of spiking temperatures, the famous map of an America castrated of its Florida by the coming rise in sea level. But the picture Adam painted was even darker than Al Gore's, because the planet is heating up so much faster than even the pessimists expected ten years ago. Adam cited the recent snowless start of the Iditarod, the sickeningly hot winter that Alaska was having, the possibility of an ice-free North Pole in the summer of 2020. He noted that whereas, ten years ago, only eighty-seven percent of the Antarctic Peninsula's glaciers were known to be shrinking, the figure now seems to be a hundred percent. But his darkest point was that climate scientists, being scientists, must confine themselves to making claims that have a high degree of statistical probability. When they model future climate scenarios and predict the rise in global temperature, they have to pick a lowball temperature, one reached in ninety-plus percent of all cases, rather than the temperature that's reached in the average scenario. Thus, the scientist who confidently predicts a five-degree (Celsius) warming by the end of the century might tell you in private, over beers, that she really expects it to be nine degrees.

Thinking in Fahrenheit—sixteen degrees—I felt very sad for the penguins. But then, as so often happens in climate-change discussions when the talk turns from diagnosis to remedies, the darkness became the blackness of black comedy. Sitting in the lounge of a ship burning three and a half gallons of fuel per minute, we listened to Adam extol the benefits of shopping at farmers' markets and changing our incandescent bulbs to LED bulbs. He also suggested that universal education for women would lower the global birth rate, and that ridding the world of war would free up enough money to convert the global economy to renewable energy. Then he called for questions or comments. The climate-change skeptics weren't interested in arguing, but a believer stood up to say that he managed a lot of residential properties, and that he'd noticed that his federally subsidized tenants always kept their homes too hot in the winter and too cold in the summer, because they didn't pay for their utilities, and that one way to combat climate change would be to make them pay. To this, a woman quietly responded, "I think the ultrawealthy waste far more than people in subsidized housing." The discussion broke up quickly after that—we all had bags to pack.

At six o'clock, the lounge filled up again, more tightly, for the climax of the expedition: the screening of a slide show to which passengers had been invited to contribute their three or four finest images. The photography instructor who was hosting it apologized in advance to anyone who didn't like the songs he'd chosen for its soundtrack. The music—"Here Comes the Sun," "Build Me Up, Buttercup"—certainly didn't help. But the whole show was dispiriting. There was the sense of diminishment I always get from our culture of images: no matter how finely you chop life into a sequence of photographs, no matter how closely in time the photographs are spaced, what the sequence always ends up conveying to me most strongly is what it leaves out. It was also sadly evident that three weeks of National Geographic instruction hadn't produced National Geographic freshness of vision. And the cumulative effect was painfully wishful. The slide show purported to capture an adventure we'd had as a community, like the community of Shackleton and his men. But there had been no long Antarctic winter, no months of sharing seal meat. The vertical relationship between Lindblad and its customers had been too insistent to encourage the forging of horizontal bonds. And so the slide show came off as an amateur commercial for Lindblad. Its wishful context spoiled even the images that should have mattered to me, the way any amateur photograph matters: by recording the face of what we love. When my brother privately showed me a picture he'd taken of Chris and Ada sitting in a Zodiac (Chris failing to maintain complete disgruntlement, Ada outright smiling), it reminded me of my happiness at having found them on the ship. The picture was full of meaning—to me. Upload it onto Lindblad's website, and its meaning collapses into advertising.

So what had been the point of coming to Antarctica? For me, it turned out, the point was to experience penguins, be blown away by the scenery, make some new friends, add thirty-one bird species to my life list, and celebrate my uncle's memory. Was this enough to justify the money and the carbon it had cost? You tell me. But the slide show did perform a kind of backhanded service, by directing my attention to all the unphotographed minutes I'd been alive on the trip—how much better it was to be bored and frozen by seawatching than to be dead. A related service emerged the next morning, after the *Orion* had docked in Ushuaia and Tom and I were set free to wander the streets by ourselves. I discovered that three weeks on the *Orion*, looking at the same faces every day, had made me intensely receptive to any face that hadn't been on it, especially to the younger ones. I felt like throwing my arms around every young Argentine I saw.

It's true that the most effective single action that most human beings can take, not only to combat climate change but to preserve a world of biodiversity, is to not have children. It may also be true that nothing can stop the logic of human priority: If people want meat and there are krill for the taking, krill will be taken. It may even be true that penguins, in their resemblance to children, offer the most promising bridge to a better way of thinking about species endangered by the human logic: They, too, are our children. They, too, deserve our care.

And yet to imagine a world without young people is to imagine living on a Lindblad ship forever. My godmother had had a life like that, after her only child was killed. I remember the half-mad smile with which she once confided to me the dollar value of her Wedgwood china. But Fran had been nutty even before Gail died; she'd been obsessed with a biological replica of herself. Life is precarious, and you can crush it by holding on too tightly, or you can love it the way my godfather did. Walt lost his daughter, his war buddies, his wife, and my mother, but he never stopped improvising. I see him at a piano in South Florida, flashing his big smile while he banged out old show tunes and the widows at his complex danced. Even in a world of dying, new loves continue to be born.

XING PED

We're told that, as a species, human beings are hardwired to take the short view, to discount a future that may never come anyway; this is certainly the thinking of the engineers who compose the traffic instructions that are painted on city streets. They seem to presume that you're driving with your eyes fixed on a spot directly beyond the hood of your vehicle. You're supposed to be like: Oh, now, there's a PED . . . and now, whoa, here comes a XING (which looks Chinese but isn't) . . . and then—well, here things become somewhat incoherent, because, if you're taking such an extremely short view, how are you even supposed to see a pedestrian who's starting to cross the street? It's weird. When you learn to drive, you're told to aim high with your steering. But if you see a message in the distance and you read it in the normal top-to-bottom way, as BUS TO YIELD, you are making a mistake. The furiously merging bus is expecting *you* to yield. Only a bad driver would know this from reading what's painted on the road. And so, to survive in a modern world in which not only traffic engineering but our reigning political and economic systems reward shortsightedness, you learn to think, or to not think, like a bad driver. You YIELD TO BUS. You take the paper cup, you drink your drink, you throw the cup away. Every minute in America, thirty thousand paper cups are chucked. Far away, on another continent, the Brazilian Atlantic rain forest has been leveled to create vast eucalyptus plantations to supply the world with pulp, but that's way beyond the hood of your vehicle. You have places much nearer you need to be. Your life is complicated enough already without dragging a reusable cup around with you all day. Even if you carried one, you know you're living in a world designed for bad drivers, and what earthly difference is your 0.00015 discarded Starbucks cups per minute going to make? What difference does it make if the emissions of your vehicle are infinitesimally hastening the arrival of an all but uninhabitable and not so distant future? Human beings are human beings, and hardwiring is hardwiring. We'll X that bridge when we come to it.